Hunger For the Hustle 1

HUNGER FOR THE HUSTLE
PRESS

Hunger for The Hustle:

Volume 1

A Collection of 28 Stories

To Inspiring You

From Struggle to Success

Collated by Jacob Fowler & Michael Bridgman

Special Thanks:

To all of our Authors and especially

Irene Lihaven

We love you and you're *Amazing!*

COLLATED BY
MICHAEL BRIDGMAN & JACOB FOWLER

HUNGER
FOR THE
HUSTLE

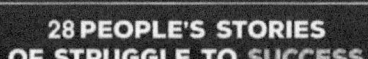

**28 PEOPLE'S STORIES
OF STRUGGLE TO SUCCESS**

Copyright © 2022 Hunger for the Hustle Press LTD

All rights reserved. No part of this publication may be reproduced, distributed, or transmitted in any form or by any means, including photocopying, recording, or other electronic or mechanical methods, without the prior written permission of the publisher, except in the case of brief quotations embodied in critical reviews and certain other non-commercial uses permitted by copyright law. For permission requests, write to the publisher at the address below.

Cover art design and creation by Luisa Arango - @arangoluisa888

First digital edition December 2022

Hunger for the Hustle Press

305/245 St Kilda Road,

Melbourne 3182

Victoria, Australia.

www.hungerforthehustle.com

A note to the reader

This book has been carefully curated over the past 2 years for you're benefit. You'll find stories inside from people all over the world, from all walks of life. Each of them has something to share with you.

Every single one of them holds some value for you. Some may evoke, joy, compassion, inspiration or admiration...

Some may ignite a spark within you that gives you a solution to that problem your trying to solve...

Some may inspire you to give some advice to a family member, friend or colleague on a challenge they are currently facing...

Some may get your creative juices flowing and give you inspiration to start a new project, business or side hustle...

With this is mind we recommend you have something close by to take notes with whilst reading this book. So you can capture those light bulb moments when they come to you.

We hope you enjoy every single word.

Michael Bridgman & Jake Fowler - Co-editor's & Co-creator's

Contents

Foreword:

Chapter 1: Broken But Never Beaten - **Beata Seweryn-Reid**

Chapter 2: From Fury to Freedom - **Janet Mackay**

Chapter 3: Life Got Better Once I Swapped the Tie For a Cape - **Jay Reace**

Chapter 4: Mama You Got This - **Jade Westlake**

Chapter 5: The Night I Slayed My Enemy In the Church Parking Lot - **Lori Bruton**

Chapter 6: "Adversity" Introduces A Person To Themselves - **Nelson Beltijar**

Chapter 7: Face Your Goliath - **Chucky Smiley**

Chapter 8: Well-Armed To Win - **Aaron Gryder**

Chapter 9: How Losing My Job Helped Me Find My Life - **Katie Corbett**

Chapter 10: Fiction Turned Real Life - **Michelle Tamiko Hardy**

Chapter 11: A Quest to Find Your Purpose - **Beanie Mann**

Chapter 12: Your Journey Has Purpose - Do What You Love - **Luis Sandoval**

Chapter 13: Landing in the Land of Plenty - **Jacob Fowler**

Chapter 14: Chase Your Dreams - **Tarnya Cowley**

Chapter 15: The Sneaky Lie That Holds Entrepreneurs Back - **Michael Bridgman**

Chapter 16: Knock Out the Unexpected Opponent - **Eric Collier**

Chapter 17: Keeping it on the Rails - **Keith Lloyd**

Chapter 18: From GED to PHD - **Dr. David A. Spencer**

Chapter 19: A Prescription for Joy & Happiness - **Fernanda Castañeda**

Chapter 20: The Courageous Queen - **Joanna Kleier**

Chapter 21: Bali Daze (Smiling Inside & Out) - **Susan Russell**

Chapter 22: From the Streets to Success - **Larry Normille**

Chapter 23: The Far Country - **Kassundra "Dr K" Brown**

Chapter 24: Re-Built & Brilliant - **Wayne Johnson**

Chapter 25: The Secret to Happiness - **Denise Nicholson**

Chapter 26: The Struggle is Real, But So is Your Greatness - **Barry Overton**

Chapter 27: A Million to Zero and Back Again in 365 Days - **Catherine Molloy**

Chapter 28: The Ultimate Rebirth - **Imani Capri**

HUNGER FOR THE HUSTLE

VOLUME 1

Foreword:

Success is a pretty funny thing. Most people work their entire lives to find it, while some people simply luck into it. But success does not come without work. While that might be a pretty obvious statement, too many people fail to understand this. New get-rich-quick schemes pop up every day, and with social media, it is even easier to fall into those traps. Watching people fall into their dreams accidentally is sometimes hard to watch, but the truth is that they are the exception, not the rule. 99.9% of the time, success comes from getting your hands dirty, putting the work in, and hustling as hard as you can.

The journey truly is the most rewarding part of the strive for success. While the results can be the stuff of dreams, there is something about the journey that keeps us coming back. If you pay attention to the successful people around you, you will notice that they are ALWAYS hustling. It isn't a job to them, but a way of life. The struggle for success is addicting, and while the end rewards are sweet, the hustle provides a high unlike any other. Seeing the fruits of your hard work pay off in real-time creates an incredible sense of accomplishment, and you will soon realize you can't quit it.

The book in your hands is a collection of incredible stories, morals, and lessons. Each contributor to this book has poured their heart and soul into every word, and their knowledge has created a wonderful piece of art. The pages ahead are exactly that, an inspiring and motivating piece of art showcasing the rise from struggle to success.

Hunger for the Hustle will not fail to move you. We all struggle in unique ways, and every author of this book has faced demons different from everybody else. No two experiences are a carbon copy, but the truth is we can all rise from the ashes. Each author conquered their hardships and ultimately found success in their struggles. My hope is that you can do the same.

A theme we talk about a lot is that success looks different to different people. What we view as a personal success may vary drastically from your perspective of success. For some people, moving their family out of a poor neighborhood is the ultimate success. Others may dream of starting a business, finding financial freedom, or even keeping healthy relationships. Just like we all struggle in different ways, we all have unique definitions of success. That's what makes life so beautiful, and so worth living.

We are confident that this book will both motivate and inspire you to begin your hustle for success. This is not just a collection of letters and words, but a gleaming beacon of hope for those lost in the struggles of an unfair life. I know you will feel moved by this book. Proceeds from the sale of this book will go to Beanie's arc. A charity that is funding research into better and kinder treatment to prevent any more very young children from dying from a really rare form of cancer called rhabdomyosarcoma. So please know that not only will your life be changed through this book, but hopefully, their lives as well.

It is a great honor and privilege that we have had the opportunity to work with those power voices that are included in this book, and we encourage all of you to find and use your voice to transform and change lives all over the world.

-Les Brown & Jon Talarico

Let the Stories Begin...

Broken But Never Beaten

By Beata Seweryn-Reid

"It's easy to hear the voices of others and often very difficult to hear your own. Every person you meet is going to want something different from you. The question is: what do you want for yourself?" – **Beyoncé Knowles**

I never wanted to be normal, so God hit me with a car.

It's interesting looking back on it now. Now, in a moment of stillness when I think about the accident, I don't remember the sounds of the screeching tires as the truck careened toward my father and me. I can't recall the smells of the leaking auto fluids or the burnt tires that left long streaks on the pavement. Even the trip to the hospital has faded in my memory.

But what still remains clear today, what has been all too vivid for many years now, are the words that were said to me by all of those who surrounded me in the weeks and months following the crash.

I had suffered a serious brain injury on that sunny fall day in 1985. The doctors' prognosis was very limited in terms of my potential to live a normal life. My health restrictions were endless, and they all started with "YOU CANNOT."

"You cannot be like the other kids anymore. You cannot expect too much from yourself. You cannot be stressed. You cannot be excited. You cannot...You cannot!" I was told that I would not be able to play like the other kids and that I shouldn't get too excited. Then there were my teachers. Those who were meant to educate me instead told me about my limitations. I wouldn't learn like the other kids. I wouldn't be able to read as well as everyone else. And when I got older, I wouldn't be able to get a good job like the other students.

For many years, these words were like old recordings in my head. I hated them (the words, not the people.) Every time I went to the doctor for a checkup, I prayed for him to say, "You are fine. Go and do great things." That permission never came from him.

And I didn't give it to myself for years either.

Looking back now, I realize that all of the people in my life had good intentions and wanted only to protect me. However, what they didn't know at the time, what they couldn't know, was that their words would stay with me for years. All those beliefs were not my own and certainly were not how I thought and felt. But over time, I believed what I had been told. After all, these were all authority figures and loved ones in my life. Why shouldn't I trust them?

In the years following the accident, I went on to become a great student, attending a great university and earning a master's degree. I followed my passion for travel by working for some of the top hotels in Poland and in the U.S. I met a wonderful man and got engaged. I was living my life regardless of the restrictions that had been imposed on me as a child.

Until the day that my fiancé walked away. On that day, all of the "you cannots" came flooding back. They were all still there, buried deep, but there. As my mind rehashed all of those limitations, I fell into a deep depression. The doctors, teachers, and relatives were right. I would never do the many things I dreamed of doing.

But I will never forget something my mother said during this tragic time as I was lamenting the fact that I wanted to be normal like everybody else. My mother with compassion, my mother with understanding, my mother, wanting to inspire and encourage me said, "Kochanie", she said, "baby, you do not want to be like everybody else, because you are not normal. You are special. You are extraordinary. You are God's miracle child." I was young and there I was with the limited visions of myself put there by everyone else - the doctors, family, society...but my mother when she spoke, because of her maturity, because of her inspiration, when she spoke, and the conviction with which she spoke, she freed me up from the limiting thoughts that had been imposed on me. I did not reply to my mom that day but in my heart, I made a statement. "Mom, I will make you proud." You see, it was then that I finally truly realized that none of the things those well-intentioned people had told me were actually true. I believed in the limitations for years, but in that moment, my mother freed me from those false stories.

Now, I was in an actual car accident. But how many of you feel like you have been in an emotional car wreck? Maybe it was when you were busy planning your future and your loved one was diagnosed with cancer. Or maybe it was when your marriage began to fail. Or when COVID came, and you lost the job to which you have dedicated your life.

This thing called life can make you BITTER or can make you BETTER. You can GO through it or you can GROW through it. Let me tell you a little secret. That thing that you are experiencing - it is not going to leave you until you grow through it. **Did you catch that? You cannot just GO through life. No! No! No! You have to GROW through it.** And growing - true personal development - often comes in the form of facing our limiting beliefs - about ourselves, about our capabilities, about our past choices and even our thoughts of the future - understanding them, and then tossing them aside. Simply because these beliefs were placed on you doesn't mean they define you. You get to choose your beliefs about yourself, those around you, and this world we share.

"Life is not a problem to be solved, but a reality to be experienced," and to experience life you need to develop the courage to change. There are three qualities that will help you to build the courage to change and to face your limiting beliefs.

First, you have to have a decisive mindset. As you look at yourself, as you look at your life and as you look at your circumstances, I want you to imagine the following. What would your life be like, what would your life look like if you DECIDED not to care about other people's opinions? What would your life be like if you DECIDED to give up some of your fears? What would your life be like if you DECIDED to be courageous and act on your dreams? In one of my favorite movies, "The Pursuit of Happiness", Will Smith plays Chris Gardner and says to his son, "*You got a dream, you gotta protect it. When people can't do something themselves, they are going to tell you that you can't do it. You want something, go get it. Period.*" This decisiveness will break through many of the false limitations you have been carrying for far too long.

Second, you need to take responsibility. As Les Brown often says, "*If you take responsibility for yourself, you will develop a hunger to accomplish your dreams.*"

You have to take ownership for your life, for your past, present and future. You have to accept that what got you *here* won't get you *there* - and it is you who can change it. So, whatever happens, take responsibility. For years, other people have told you - even you have told yourself - what you can accomplish. Ask yourself, "*Is this true?*" Then move forward with your newfound responsibility to live fully.

Third, you need a vision. Helen Keller said, "*The only thing worse than being blind is having sight but no vision.*" I do not know you but because you are reading this, it tells me that there is something in you that is greater than your circumstances. There is something in you that is greater than the adversity that you are facing. It tells me that you do have a vision for yourself, for your family, for your community. Your vision IS your dream. The dream that you had before the world told you what was possible for you. Have the courage to follow your dreams. Start where you are. Use what you have. And do not stop until you get there. "Do not let people without a vision convince you that your vision is impossible. However, it is entirely possible, that they are wrong."

Martin Luther King, Jr. said, "*You don't have to see the whole staircase, just take the first step.*" Your first step is to begin to recognize and face the limiting beliefs. And not just the ones put on you by parents, teachers, or coaches, but the stories you have been telling yourself for many years. Once you realize not only that these stories aren't true, but also that you get to write your own story, you will begin to see and feel the possibilities all around you. What I once thought of as a tragic day so many years ago has turned into a blessing. I was gifted with the realization that we get to write our own story. And with this truth, go and write the best novel you can envision.

From Fury to Freedom

Discovering Your Purpose – Stop Looking and Start Being!

By Janet Mackay

My search for purpose tormented me!

All throughout my life, this relentless feeling that there was so much more to life, had caused fury in my soul. Fury, that was not acceptable to show or talk about. I would question it so often in my mind growing up, as I saw my mother struggling as a single parent, having gone through a bitter divorce, living on food stamps, and continuously reminding my brother and I that these were the cards that had been dealt for us. I called, "Bullshit!"

I learned my role in the family chain at a young age. I was the happy, cheerful, full of energy one and the one who was always able to shift the mood of a room from negative to positive. I was the responsible one who always figured it all out. I was the one who always saw the positive, even in the ugliest of situations. I was the one who believed in the magic of Santa Claus and found wonder and awe all around me. These became my superpowers!

We moved in with my grandparents when I entered High School. My grandfather was a stern and very wise man who I always had a connection with. I appreciated the "structure" and his perfection to everything he did, and it inspired me to work harder to achieve more and win his accolades. I graduated from a private college in Boston, landed some amazing career opportunities, traveled for business, obtained an MBA and was able to purchase expensive gifts to bring home for my family! I got married, have two phenomenal children and three stepchildren and was successful at blending two families. I made people proud!

Yet, with all of that, I was still tormented by my unrelenting true search for purpose. From the outside, no one would have ever known. I vividly remember a night, after drinking at a party, (something I did often,) falling to my knees alone in my backyard, looking up at the darkened sky, with the moon shining bright and begging, "*God, please tell me my reason for being, I need to know, please tell me*", as tears were streaming down my face.

But, unlike the movies, there was no booming voice or strike of lightning following my plea. I heard nothing.

If I was placed here on purpose for a purpose, then why was I still searching and why did it ache so much?

When you ask anyone what they want most out of life, do you know what the top three answers are?

#1: They want to be happy.

#2: They want to be a part of something, to feel connected, and know that they matter.

#3: They want to make an impact.

My journey started as I began to find these answers for myself.

I dove even deeper into personal development. I grew stronger in learning about the power of the mind and energy. I let go of preconceived rules about religion and found a spiritual home that helped me build a relationship with God and a better understanding of scripture. What I had deemed as my superpowers were all starting to make some sense, and the bountiful energy I naturally possessed was the strongest force. I found this to be true when I **stopped searching and started "being", learning it wasn't all about me!**

This positive energy was my #1 superpower, and it became my mission for the whole world to feel its magnificence! The vision on how to share this was downloaded to me as, "The Power of the DRIP!" I know it sounds wonky, so let me explain!

It is a scientific fact that we are all energy. That the world is energy, and that we emit energy, feel energy and absorb energy and that our thoughts, feelings and words have energy.

Here is an exercise to demonstrate this. Please position your hands together as if you are holding an imaginary large rubber ball, (fingers not touching). Close your eyes and inhale deeply and exhale strongly, and while you do this, push against the imaginary sphere between your hands. Continue this practice for a few minutes. Focus on your breathing as you are pushing against this imaginary sphere, and the feeling that is happening. You will begin to feel an energy between your hands and perhaps even some tingling in your fingers!

Now picture a small drip of water dangling from a green leaf hovering over a puddle after a big rain. Watch it as it falls. What happens when that drip of water hits that puddle below? What do you see, what do you hear? Do you see how it creates a ripple upon impact, whose movement continues outward, expanding ring, by ring, by ring?

Since YOU are energy, and when your thoughts, your actions, and your words act as DRIPS that show kindness, compassion, connection and gratitude towards others, the energy released will create a ripple of positive energy that in turn, will make an INPact on the life of another. (Here it is spelt I-N-P-A-C-T to define it as an intentional positive action). The intentional choice to jump in to be a "A Drip That Rips, and Not A Drop That Plops!"

I experienced the power of the drip first-hand and its amazing energy, while directing children's summer camps over the past fourteen years.

As I shared this with others and made it a part of our training and culture; kids, adults and businesses were stepping forward to share how they were making their own INPact in the world. I felt a tug on my heart to then use my platform to interview and showcase these amazing stories and share them with others:

- Jillian, a twelve-year-old girl learns about a teacher in her school who has a son with special abilities who desperately wanted to ride a bicycle, however required an adaptive tricycle that was very expensive. Upon hearing this, Jillian gathers a few friends and on their own, raises the money to present their teacher with a check so she can purchase the bicycle for her son so he can learn to ride, "Drip....... ripple!"

- Tobie, a mom from Utah starts a non-profit foundation bringing teens and young adults on trips to serve people in Guatemala, often bringing with her 2,000 backpacks filled with supplies and food to hand out to families, "Drip.... ripple!"

- Alex, the owner of an entertainment company who shifts his business to teach kids and young adults with special abilities to learn how to become DJ's. Kids with autism who were non-verbal, who, when put in front of a microphone and hit record, would speak! "Drip.... ripple!"

- Jeremy, a young adult, sees a man shivering while sitting on his flattened box so he starts a coat drive and distributes over 1,000 coats to the homeless throughout the streets of NYC, "Drip.... ripple!"

When I stopped searching and started serving, I was able to identify that which lit my soul on fire! My purpose became clear when I stopped seeking approval and accolades from others and started celebrating the good I saw in people. I am here to teach and inspire others to find what lights them up from the inside and show them how to use their gifts to serve others. I am here as a vehicle to share stories of INPact found throughout the world. I am here as an Ambassador for Positive Change!

The beautiful part in all of this, is the shift I saw in the people close to me. The person I once called "Bullshit" on, is one of them. My amazing mom, who has since burned those cards of life she thought she had been dealt. She now realizes that living in daily gratitude is the best hand to be dealt, and she's now living with a joyful heart with abundance all around her.

If you are still struggling to find your purpose, spend time getting to know who created you. Stop searching and start being. Use the tools available to strengthen your mindset and know that all change starts, "one...drip...at...a...time!" The ripples you create, will continue to move outward, ring by ring and connect with others, who are doing the same. And I promise you, it will answer the question I shared earlier. As those ripples connect, we will create a tsunami of global kindness and compassion that will be felt throughout the world. From there, you will feel the joy and connection in your heart knowing you are making a positive difference in the lives of many!

My search for purpose no longer torments me. As Mark Twain stated, *"the two most important days in your life are the day you were born and the day you find out why."* The journey taught me that I had been living within my purpose the whole time, as I used my gifts and tapped into my superpowers. Celebrate your journey, it is unique to you for a reason. Use your gifts to "Make an INPact," to keep those ripples moving. Utilize the platforms you have. Most importantly, share what you have learned today with those around you, especially our children, who make up 40% of our population, but make up 100% of our future!

You were magnificently created!! Be the change YOU want to see in the world... YOU can make it happen:

One

Drip

At

A

Time!

The world needs your greatness now, more than ever!

Life Got Better Once I Swapped the Tie for a Cape

By Jay Reace

At what age do we stop believing in our abilities to dream and reach for the unattainable? Is it the moment our innocence starts to fade or is it the moment an adult feels we are old enough to put behind us childish things and learn their truth and inherit their fears? For a long time in my life, I felt I was searching for something. Something I was missing. Something that would make me happy and give my life purpose. Unbeknownst to me I already had it within.

You see, my parents are divorced. And to cope, I would often use my imagination to create whole worlds full of people and events. Envisioning sold out concerts to hundreds as I entertained. I'd hold the attention of millions while speaking with conviction, as I gave a captivating speech. And when I wasn't performing or giving a great speech, I would pretend I was the superhero Mr. Positivity, killing the negative vibes of this world with kindness and an upbeat attitude, all while making it a better place for all.

From an early age I loved heroes and I believe the creator instilled superpowers deep within all of us. Now, I know how juvenile that may sound. And some might be hesitant to believe they have superpowers. But I get it, after all I'm telling you, you have superpowers, something kids often believe fictional characters have.

Ironically, it's when we're children we discover our superpowers. However, somewhere along the way, we lose connection to them. Because as adults we think superpowers are these unimaginable grandiose things, when in fact superpower is defined as having the great ability to do or act, not shoot lasers from your eyes or blow freeze breath from your lips, but in doing what you are meant to do.

For me, I was meant to use my imagination to create, because as a kid my superpower was my imagination and unfortunately that made me different, I would often stand out in a crowd because of my adventurous imagination. And unfortunately, not everyone was understanding of my super ability to imagine and create. One day my father sat me down and told me in a very loving, caring voice,

"Son, you should tone things down and be more like water. See water is flexible and can be what everyone, needs it to be. I need you to be like water and tone it down."

Now, I believe my father meant nothing by his comment but, he projected his fears onto me, and I merely ran with it. Becoming like water and disconnecting myself from my imagination. I stopped letting my creativity flow out, so I wouldn't stand out. And in turn, began the process of losing myself and my great abilities. I didn't know this at that time, but it's those closest to us that are often those who introduce villains into our lives. Because that was my introduction to the villain, Conformity.

Conformity would grow to become the Joker to my Batman. However, unlike Batman, I wasn't putting up a fight. For years, I stayed in line, conformed with no imagination. And traveled down a path of losing who I was and who I should have been. I had stopped dreaming. I had become, dare I say… ordinary. I was literally living an ordinary life, in every ordinary way. To put it simply, I was living beneath my potential and all because I chose to conform and got in line with every other victim choosing to be ordinary.

Conformity ruled over my life with an iron fist, keeping me in line. I got in line for a 9 to 5 job, I hated. I got in line for the "POWER TIE" that had no power, other than keeping me tied to my desk. I even got in line for fruitless conversations, about pointless things to impress powerless people. I was in that line for so long, I became exhausted and didn't realize I was burnt out. I found myself depressed and having suicidal thoughts.

In those dark moments of my life, I had given up my powers to imagine. I'd given up my dreams to inspire. I lost connection with myself. And I needed to find how to get me back. I began working on figuring out who I was. It was in those dark moments of pain and despair; I had a choice to make. I could continue to fear everything and run or face everything and rise.

I chose to rise.

Because in my pain and misery of conforming to worldly standards, I realized water is powerful.

Yes, water is flexible, but water can be unstoppable. With enough force and pressure, water can burst through any substance. It was at this point I realized the power I held inside and decided to jump out of line.

Having superpowers doesn't mean leaping off of tall buildings. It's facing the fear of leaving the familiar. Which can feel a lot like leaping off of a tall building when faced with the unknown. But imagine being comfortable in our situations, regardless of the pain or stress we may be having in it. We don't want to leave it. Because, until the pain of our current situation is greater than the fear of leaving it, things won't change. So, we must find the courage to leap off the building of conformity and soar into our destiny.

After all, if we fear the fall, we will never know what it is to fly. Now, I'm not implying soaring into your destiny is easy, because life will have its own unique way of catching us off guard. However, like any true compelling tale, when life knocks you down, you must rise up and be the hero, in the dark chapters of your life. Standing up with conviction and courage against the villains that stand in the way of you achieving your dreams. But before we go any further. I would like to ask you,

"Who are you? Can you tell me more than your name?" I only ask because, in my dark moments, I didn't know who I really was, beyond my own name. Because I was and possibly even you, are still in line. Most people don't take the time to look inside and defeat their own inner traumas.

As I write this, the current state of the world is about nine months into the Covid-19 pandemic and people are losing their minds. Because for the first time, they are forced to face the demons inside them. And until we face ourselves intentionally, the external villains will win. An old African proverb says, if you defeat the enemy within, no enemy without can harm you. So harness the superpowers within and become the hero of your story to vanquish the villains of your life. Now, I jumped out of line by looking in the mirror and reminding myself, to just be me... JUST BE YOU.

So, when you think about your dreams, decide to act on them and jump out of line. Be reborn and aspire for your greatness because you were born for greatness. Your superpowers are inside you. Regardless of your responsibilities or adversity you can achieve your greatness. I decided I was going to act and began developing myself, expanding my skills, living a larger life for myself, and my family, so we can live a life of legacy.

I decided to say, it's possible to go after my dreams to become who I envisioned. I decided to stop searching for what was already inside me and say yes to the superpowers within me to create the stories I saw in my mind. I honed my abilities to create fiction, I trained to tell tantalizing tales, I dove deep to resolve my repressed trauma and I grappled with loosening conformities grasp, to find my greatest power and strength.

The superpower of hope, hope can be a challenging strength to come by. Particularly when things aren't going the way you expect or when you are in a place that seems impossible to come out of.

See, I was in that place for so long and, at times it felt my dreams were impossible. But I would remember what Nelson Mandela said, *"Everything is impossible until it's done"*. So, I jumped out of line, leaving the familiar shadow of conformity, and said yes to my 2nd superpower, imagination. This, in turn, was saying yes to my greatness.

So anytime you start to doubt yourself tell yourself, it's possible. Because it doesn't matter what your superpowers are. If you are an entrepreneur, no matter the circumstance, you can start that dream business. If you had to leave school early, you can go back and get that degree. If you are an artist, you can create the next masterpiece.

There is someone waiting to be saved by your superpowers. There are people waiting for you to jump out of line and find who you are meant to be. Start believing in your abilities to dream and reach for the unattainable. Start embracing your truth, ignore the fears of others and live in your power. Because, when you are true to you and live in your power, you act on your dreams, and become who you were destined to be. For a long time in my life, I lost my power to imagine and in turn, who I was destined to be. I felt I was searching for something I was missing. Unbeknownst to me I already had it within. The power to make myself happy and the ability to give my own life purpose. I learned to live in my own power. Saying yes to myself, just as you are. Harness your superpowers and jump out of line. Live the life you were called to live and build your legacy.

But before you go, I love helping and hearing about those living in their power and building a legacy of their own. Please, reach out and or connect with me via social media at "@iamjayreace" currently on Facebook[1], Twitter[2], Instagram[3], and or Tiktok.[4]

---

1. https://www.facebook.com/jay.reace.39

2. https://mobile.twitter.com/findingjayreace/

3. https://www.instagram.com/findingjayreace/

4. https://www.tiktok.com/@findingjayreace

Mama, You Got This

By Jade Westlake

Motherhood... The most wonderful, rewarding and magical feeling to experience, being empowered with such a lot of love for a little life you have created.

Upon finding out I was pregnant a whole surge of emotions ran through me. SO many questions that still even now I don't necessarily know the answers to were running through my mind, it sent me into overdrive and overwhelm. There is a perception (or at least I felt there was) of how I should be as a mother. How I should act, how I should feel, and how I should always do my best in every way I could. Excitement and fear are two of the strongest emotions that I experienced a lot throughout my pregnancy and in my first year of becoming a mum. I know they may sound far away from each other but for me they felt closely connected. I used to run from fear and do anything I could to block it out. Since being a mother to my beautiful boy, I now feel more confident than ever before. Now I face fear head on and when facing struggles, they no longer scare me like they used to because I know just like the story I'm about to tell you they will only make me stronger, and better equipped to deal with life's challenges.

I am the type of women who like's to be **organised**. Sometimes if I'm honest with you, perhaps a little bit too organised. Organisation is important to me it makes me happy, it keeps me calm, and in this fast-paced world we live in, it keeps me sane! Those that know me well know my diary is never far away and that I always try to schedule life at least a week ahead. This is who I am and I wouldn't have it any other way, but sometimes I feel that it stops me being present and from living in the moment.

I promised myself I would work on this flaw, and in particular really try to be the best version of myself, to in turn be the best mother I possibly be. I never wanted to miss a moment or miss a milestone because I was too caught up in something else. One thing I was certain on is that I wanted to bring my son into a world that he felt loved, nurtured, and cared for. That anything he wanted was possible and that no matter what... he always felt my love and my presence.

In October 2019 my world changed forever and nothing as I knew it would ever be the same again. I became a Mama! I remember looking at my son in total awe. Waiting for his first cry felt like an eternity but sure enough when it came, I could feel my heart bursting with happiness.

My standout memory leading up to giving birth was why is it whenever people talk about their labour, they always tell you the horror story's before the beautiful ones? I was inundated with stories and fear crept in. However, working through these negative feelings and thoughts instead of becoming consumed by them. Helped me to create my own mindset and my own vision of how I wanted my labour to be. After all, their stories are their own just as mine are my own.

I spent a lot of time hypnobirthing which equipped with the simple breathing techniques that really helped to keep me calm, focused and push past the fear and pain of childbirth. I didn't choose to attend antenatal classes and although I don't doubt, they are helpful I personally never really felt I missed out. They seemed a bit textbook to me... and I don't like texts books. Any mothers reading this will know that no amount of reading or research can really prepare you for the journey of motherhood. It's a journey that's driven by instinct and intuition. Most of what I did especially in my son's first few days, weeks and months was driven by my caring intuition, my motherly instinct, and my developing ability to understand my baby's needs and wants.

I especially loved the night times, not so much for the sleep deprivation (which by the way I'm sure is a form of torture!) But for the pure, calm, peaceful feeling I received knowing the world is silent and sleeping but I am needed. I often wondered who else was awake in the world and I'd treasure these moments so much because as tiring as they were, they gave me the time to have a pure uninterrupted connection with my boy, to make our bond even deeper, and to reflect. My son needed me, he was hungry and every few hours he certainly had no problem letting me know! This was defining moment in my journey of motherhood in which I felt **so** needed, more needed than I'd ever felt before. I've never quite felt an emotion like the one of feeling needed in those moments. It is one of such significance that nothing can truly compare to. In those small quiet hours of the morning, I basked in my son's need for me, as I held him in my arms and held his gaze with my eyes.

As the days and weeks passed following the birth of my son and I started to heal both emotionally and physically. I found the want and desire to meet other mums and begin my journey with those I could relate to a little more. I attended local baby classes which took me an awful lot of confidence to step out of my comfort zone and adapt to the new topics of conversation. Slowly but surely, I began to embrace this whole new chapter of life and I adored it. Watching our babies meet and interact whilst sharing the stories of motherhood just felt so natural to me, and knowing I was so unjudged and believed in helped to keep me stay calm on the days when the journey became challenging, and my head became foggy. I took the belief others had in me and transformed that energy to believe in myself.

I will never forget something my Mum said to me when I was pregnant she said *'When you become a mum you will never stop worrying'* But how lovely to worry about someone so much because you care with an endless amount of love.

2020 quickly became the year of change and as the month's past, my maternity leave was in full swing. Suddenly and seemingly out of nowhere... a worldwide pandemic hit, and I felt everything I had begun to know and learn about motherhood do a full 360 right in front of my eyes. I wanted nothing more than to protect my baby from this virus that had overcome us and turned the world as we knew it upside down. To keep him as safe as possible without passing my worry and anxious energy towards him.

This new heavily restricted way of life (lockdown as they called it) initially did not scare me, but what did scare me is that the support unit I had built. My immediate family, close friends and all the Mum's from the baby classes, Everyone I really needed was being taken from under my feet. Much like many things in life I didn't truly appreciate its value until it was gone. Some days I would wake up feeling guilty for not feeling happy, I mean I should be happy, shouldn't I? ... but I didn't, my reality was that I felt guilty for bringing my son into this strange and bewildering world. The uncertainty of what the future would hold, and if it would ever return to normal... the fear was back again how long would it stay for this time?

I soon realised I could not maintain this unhealthy train of thought and instead of letting the situation define me, I would define it. I used it to empower me and make the most of every single day. I'm not saying this was easy, motherhood quickly became very lonely and hard to enjoy. I began questioning myself and my abilities a lot, has my baby eaten enough... slept enough... is he stimulated enough... have I done enough... did I do all the washing?!

Seeing my baby smile at the littlest things made me realise just how much joy can be found in everyday life. As time passed, I began to realise that although the pandemic was an awful life event, it became the pause in life many of us needed without even knowing it. The pause to readjust and reconnect, to rewind and relax and to cherish and to savour each moment and memory instead of taking them for granted.

The physical support bubble that had been formed in my early days of motherhood had been taken away very suddenly. Although my husband was with us on the evenings and weekends and provided endless physical and emotional support the deep loneliness would take its toll, and it quickly became apparent that the support I wanted and the support I needed from him was more emotional rather than just physical.

Just the simple odd message here and there of 'How are you today?' meant such a lot to me. Many I knew were struggling with the pressures and sudden changes that the pandemic inflicted. I wanted to do all I could to reassure others how important it is to talk. I often would message loved ones *'Here if you need me, here if you don't'.* I adopted a new mindset; I was determined to not let these circumstances and the struggles they brought define me. I refocused my energy, determined to face them head on and in this way of helping myself I hoped I could help others too, even if it was just a little. Focus goes where energy flows, and that energy can filter out to others around you near or far.

Life can be so 24/7, and we often forget the value of the moment until it's becomes a memory. I found that savouring the little quiet moments of this time. They helped me build the bond with my son immensely. In this quiet time, I also found myself scrolling through social media and through group chat discussions with my network of new mums. Although this was a support network to me, and one I was really grateful for. I found myself subconsciously comparing myself to other mums and their baby's development, many of which were baby girls which tend to be more advanced than boys. I had to stop myself in this because as excited for my boys development milestones, I learned that comparing my life to others brings no value to my own. In fact all it does is waste time and energy and counteracts what I was actively trying to get better at... **BEING PRESENT!**

My one piece of advice to other mums is to not put pressure on yourself to do this and do that. It will all come at the time it is meant too and when it does it will be beautiful to see your child grow and learn at the pace that is right for them. Trust the journey.

Still to this day I wonder if I am doing things right when in truth, there is no right. A human life is the most precious blessing in the world and one that should be never taken for granted. I learnt through the dark days that better ones will come and amidst all the uncertainty and worry, there is a lot of love to be found in the world. Show kindness and kindness will show itself to you. Becoming a new mum in a worldwide pandemic taught me **a lot**, most importantly it taught me that other people's expectations didn't matter and often weren't even there, I was just loading unneeded expectations onto myself.

The world as we know it now will always be different, it is forever changing and is the only constant. We will adapt, we will not be defined by our expectations, or by our fears, or what is set out against us, we will overcome. Through the experience of these struggles we will emerge **stronger**.

There is no perfect way to be a mother but a million ways to be a good one, it is about learning your strengths you did not know you had and dealing with fears you did not know existed. Know that amongst everything... **mama you got this, mama you are enough.**

A huge thank you to my son, Jenson Ocean. You needed me, but I needed you so much too. May you always know how loved you are.

Thank you to all my incredible Family and friends, your support then and now always means so much and you make me feel incredibly blessed and grateful.

The Night I Slayed My Enemy in a Church Parking Lot

By the LORI Factor - Lori Bruton

The darkness of that night was blinding. I sat in my car in a church parking lot with tears streaming down my face as I pounded the steering wheel. Bursting out of my car, I began walking down the sidewalk in a rage until I came to a liquor store. *How can I numb this intense pain?* Forcing a smile and hiding my tears, I grabbed a big bottle of liquor and swiftly paid for it.

The warm summer breeze and the smell of evergreen trees would've been a delight any other night. Instead, there was a cold chill inside my mind and body. Brown bag in hand, I walked back to my car oblivious of my surroundings. Sitting in the driver's seat of my parked car, I unscrewed the bottle of alcohol and let it pour into me, hoping to numb the pain. The enemy consumed me and took control.

I was going nowhere sitting in my parked car. The only thing driving now was the alcohol as I stumbled out of my car and fell onto the stones. I crawled until I passed out drunk under a truck in that church parking lot.

Prior to that night, I believed I would bring love and light to others when I signed up for the ministry training class at this church, across the street from my own. Instead, darkness fell upon me and opened doors from my past I thought were closed. Each week the instructor covered topics including death, divorce, abusive relationships, alcohol abuse, addictions, domestic violence, dysfunctional families, sexual assaults, unhappy women who had abortions, people with abandonment issues, and on and on.

Weekly, I sat on hard metal chairs in the dingy basement classroom of the church. I listened to the instructor present different scenarios and how best to respond biblically with care.

What happened to me that night was the culmination of what the instructor said, and things buried inside of me for years. I was at the training class to learn how to minister to others, be compassionate, actively listen, and help them cope and heal. Instead, my own experiences were triggered. It was difficult to focus during class as my past unfolded within me. I had experienced some of the topics discussed firsthand or witnessed others I love go through them. One night I looked out the tiny basement window and saw a rainstorm brewing. I was about to encounter the storm brewing in my mind which was much worse.

I had a beautiful loving home with a good husband and two wonderful sons. I loved my family. I was living the life I wanted. Unexpectedly, the darkness of my past crept in and devoured my happy home. Apparently, I wasn't aware that I suppressed hurtful memories and experiences that exploded out. They left a trail of destruction.

My father left our home when I was about thirteen years old and that was one of the hardest things to accept. I had to learn how to live without him there. I made some poor decisions looking for love in all the wrong places.

The instructor agreed to help me sort through my triggered memories after class. I thought things were progressing very well. He listened intently and seemed to understand me. I was filled with joy and hope as he took time to guide me through these challenges. Then the tide turned when, one night in class, with the whole group present, my emotions surfaced.

Silent tears were gushing out of me. I did my best to be discreet as I listened to his teaching. The folding chairs were in a half circle. The person next to me whispered, *"Are you okay?"* my classmates signaled the instructor to address my struggle. They were appalled that he ignored me and just let me cry as he continued to teach.

Finally, he excused himself and escorted me into another room like a naughty child. He told me he would deal with me later and said I was not allowed back in class ever again. The weight and humiliation of being banished broke me into a million pieces. I bolted from the 'naughty' room in the basement and took to the streets searching for a way to numb my pain. The path led me to that liquor store.

I couldn't take it anymore. The hurt was so intense. He promised to be there and now I was banned and thrown away like garbage. That is when the landslide occurred. That is how I ended up a broken intoxicated mess passed out drunk under his truck in that church parking lot on that ominous night.

The next thing I knew I was waking up in an ambulance with my family looking on with concern. The pain on their faces was excruciating. I wasn't capable of pulling myself together and being okay. I wanted to erase that night. My pain spilled onto those I love most.

What had I done?

That night had a domino effect on my life. I was never the same. My newfound drinking roared out of control, and I slipped into a different world. Pouring the warm liquor into me felt more comforting than the memories of my past. I was constantly confronted by the mistakes I'd made or the things I saw growing up. On top of the past, I now had the new memory of being humiliated by the class instructor. My behavior at home was different. I hadn't told my family that I began drinking, but they knew something was off.

The shame ate me up and engaging in toxic relationships became my norm. I contemplated ending my life. One day, my suicidal thoughts were too clear and the details of how I was going to end it were too convincing. I no longer listened to my plans, I acted on them. This scared me and my family. That day I told myself that I was going to do whatever it takes to stay alive and be present for my sons.

Today is a new day. I have learned to heal from the pain and not bury it. I have learned to forgive myself and the people who have hurt me. I know how to love and value myself now. I realize that life is God's gift to us, and how we live our lives is our gift to God. That Lori, who was under a truck, drunk in a church parking lot is gone. She is dead.

I embarked on a journey of rebirth discovering and developing myself to become the best version of me. This transformation resulted in extraordinary gifts emerging through faith, awareness, and belief. No longer was I under that dark spell that had me sleepwalking through life.

What lifestyle do you want? What legacy will you leave? When my earthly assignment is complete, I picture myself with a pen and paper in my hands as I float in a boat on the sea, finishing my race and touching God's face.

Every experience we go through is all part of our journey and preparation. I wanted to give up so many times, but God guided me back.

I love this quote by Les Brown, *"When life knocks you down, try to land on your back. Because if you can look up, you can get up."* I thank God that I literally landed on my back, in life. Because I could look up, I got up and am living life the Lori way. I call it The LORI Factor,

#1 L – LOOK through the Lord's loving eyes to see a larger vision of your life and create a vision of yourself beyond your circumstances and mental conditioning.

#2 O – OPTIMISM. Have an optimistic spirit and the possibility that you can change your life.

#3 R – REINVENT yourself. You've got to be willing to make radical changes in your behavior to live a purposeful life.

#4 I – INVEST in yourself. Bet on you. You're an asset to the planet.

You have something special. You have greatness in you. You're a masterpiece because you are a piece of the Master.

Slay the enemy. Create the life of your dreams. Claim your victory. I believe in you. Let's talk. Next steps: Text me at 1-844-394-4798

Find me on Facebook at: https://www.facebook.com/LoriBrutonbiz

"Adversity" Introduces a Person to Themselves

By Nelson Beltijar

I haven't walked, upright on my own, for almost 4 years - 1651 days to be exact - in fact, the last time I had fully used my legs was on June 26, "2016". That's right!!! June 26th, "2016"!!! However, everything finally changed for me on January 3rd, 2021.

On this day, I was re-born, transformed, and ready to reclaim my place back into the world, only this time, armed with sky opening epiphanies to water the seeds of the souls around me. Ladies and Gentlemen, I'm wondering if there's anyone out there who has ever had life give you something you didn't expect???

If yes, then we're kindred spirits and you'll understand, hear, and feel the following words on these upcoming pages.

"Adversity" is an inescapable earthly experience that 99.99 % of the world's population will have to go through and it truly introduces a person to themselves. My friends, I'm the kind of guy that knows what it's like to climb that mountain of ambition and success, get to the top, enjoy the view there for a while, only to come crashing down, spiralling down, losing everything that I had ever worked for in a blink of an eye. Talk about humbling... so humbling.

I was lucky enough to build a thriving Physical Therapy & Personal Training Private Practice specializing in Injury Assessment, Treatment, and Rehabilitation and I'll never forget this. It was May 2016, and we were on the second floor of my studio clinic loft celebrating. Celebrating, clanging the champagne glasses - which were secretly filled with Diet Coke or Ginger Ale - CELEBRATING and high fiving one another because we had reached a monumental goal.

However, a week later, 168 hours after that joyous moment in time, I was shockingly diagnosed with cancer and immediately admitted into the hospital for supervision, evaluation, and chemotherapy treatments for the remainder of 2016. You're not going believe this, to add salt to the wound, I even lost my ability to walk. As a secondary complication of this disease, I became a prisoner in a wheelchair for the following 3 years.

My "2017" wasn't any easier, it was filled with tumour removal surgeries, hospital discharges, in-home fainting's, 911 ambulance calls, surgical wound complications, hospital re-admissions, countless downtown Doctor(s) appointments, cancer spreading false alarms, which by the way was my favourite bump in the road, spinal infections, and in-home antibiotic IV drip treatments.

My "2017" was nothing but a blur and a year where I couldn't catch a break.

Eventually, my 2018 rolled around and it's ironic that I'm a Physical Therapist because my entire 2018 was filled with my own physical rehabilitation "project" where the goal was to graduate from my imprisoning wheelchair of 3 years into a mobile walker, then on to "2" canes, then eventually to a single cane, with the aim of triumphantly returning back to full functional ability walking on my own alongside my friends and family once again.

My friends, would be brave enough to go left when every single qualified person around you was telling and leading you to go right!

As I was forced to live in the hospitals, in 2016 & 2017, because it was no longer safe for me to stay at home, I was faced with becoming a prisoner of my own hospital bed, however, I refused to let my mind remain trapped in that hospital room.

I'd let my brain roam freely beyond the four walls of my room, and the entire hospital, as I would visualize myself out in the world living a typical Monday, Tuesday, Wednesday, Thursday, Friday Saturday, and Sunday. I would mentally see, hear, and feel myself going through a typical day, its typical errands, its typical conversations, and its typical arguments, with patients, friends, and family. You see, for almost 3 years, I would use the tool of mental imagery to trick my subconscious into believing that I was out in the world living instead of being stuck in the hospital bed dying.

Yes, the Dr's said that I was tumour filled and it was completely unsafe for me to leave the hospital and return back into my life. Yes, I heard what the doctors had said, but I refused to believe what they were telling me. Regardless of the words that they spoke, I had already made up my mind that I was going to return to the life that I had reluctantly left behind even if that meant I had to create my own fantasy of a reality within my mind.

So, that's what I did.

It was obvious to everyone that I was stubbornly refusing to accept the picture that my cancer doctors were painting of myself and my current health situation. As a result, I dug even deeper into my parallel universe and alternative form of reality and employed the technical, conquering, game skills of one of my favourite childhood pastimes.

Ladies & Gentlemen, have any of you ever played the video game called Pac Man, where the Pac Man icon eats up the dots in the game?

Well, as silly as this may sound, I would visualize that I had an internal Pac Man icon in my own body whose purpose was to gobble away all of my cancer cells. Crazy huh?

As gullible as this may sound, I tapped into the power of visualization once again during the years of 2016, 2017, and 2018 and I'd mentally see myself walking, completely upright on my own, down specific streets, surrounded by specific people, walking past specific buildings & stores, high fiving one another in celebration as we reached our symbolic finish line.

You see, I was foolish enough to believe in the impossible and I suspended my disbelief long enough to slip the principles of mental imagery and visualization into my cancer battling toolbox before doubt and skepticism had a chance to creep in.

There's a common thought that there's a mind, body, and spirit connection but to me that was just words on a page up until I totally committed to including these principles into my treatments and physical rehabilitation.

Although my professional, pre-determined, and physical hospital environment had been already established as the specific backdrop for my story to unfold, it was via the tools of mental imagery and visualization, that I was able to creatively construct my own reality and put myself in a position to Win.

As difficult as all this may sound, the above text was the "easy" part of my cancer battling journey.

On top of all of this, I was forced to "live" in "5" different hospitals from June 2016 - November 2017 and my first Cancer doctor, that's right my VERY FIRST Cancer doctor, let's call him "Dr. K", gave up on me and told my family that I was terminal and that he and the hospital could do nothing else for me and that he was going to transfer me to the Palliative Care team to ensure that I would be "comfortable" and "pain-free" in my remaining days. When I heard this, it was like a sword swooped downward and cut me at the knees and my life flashed before my eyes. After wallowing in self pity for about 10 minutes I promised myself that if I was going to die, I would go out in a bang, climb one more mountain, and chase down one last purpose filled goal before my time on Earth was done.

Instead of writing my goodbye letters, I laid in my hospital bed, staring at the ceiling, tears rolling down the right side of my face, thinking, brainstorming, and dreaming of ways of how I could contribute to the lives of my younger family members. It was then that the light bulb of my mind had switched on and it became clear to me that my last undying mission was to write a blog, a blog that contained the knowledge and life nuggets that I had acquired with my time on this planet. This blog would be my life's curtain call.

You see, at that time, I had a 6-year-old nephew, 2 nieces that were 5 and 3 years old, 2 brand newborn twins, who I loved dearly, but I also knew that I wasn't going to get a chance to see them grow up and this broke my heart. It became my yearning desire to create this blog to leave it behind for them so I could STILL be a part of their lives even after I had passed away.

But you want to hear something funny? It looks like the joke's on me.

Let's fast forward to September "2018" …

1) My brand-new cancer doctors, who fought for me and tried everything to keep me alive, miraculously stamped me cancer free and told me to go live my life.

2) That blog that I specifically created to leave behind for my younger family members has ended up trickling across the planet resulting in a global readership - which was never the plan. Crazy huh?

... and last, but not least ...

3) A global community has accidentally evolved, and is rallying around, and currently walking alongside that blog - It's so humbling and I still can't believe it. I don't tell you this brag. I share this with you to show you:

•How Adversity introduced, and converted, me into a stronger, more resilient me.

•How Adversity pulled me away from faltering and introduced me to the importance of having to fight.

•How Adversity introduced and inspired one last undying goal in me to create that love filled blog.

•How Adversity turned my mind "on" to the possibilities of what I could do in my perceived remaining days instead of turning it off.

Instead of me lying in my hospital bed waiting for the coffin to arrive, I used my perceived remaining days to accidentally create a globally impactful blog. I sincerely believe that the main reason my blog has been so well received is because I chose to invite the world into the honesty of my dark and vulnerable place allowing them to mentally sit with me. I had learned what it felt like to feel inadequate, insignificant, invisible, unheard, unseen, lost, alone, lonely, scared, and unsure. Words I never knew before, words that terrified me, and words that almost buried me and I think that it's these specific words, and my newly found feelings, that has made my blog relatable and embraceable to the masses around the globe.

The detrimental effects of cancer on my health combined with the uncertainty of my return-to-work date has put me in a very difficult and stressful situation. In a blink of an eye my everyday life, as I knew it, was taken away from me. Although I may look grinfully the same on the outside, my battle with cancer has forever changed me on the inside. As fate would have it, as a result of my physical and emotionally filled cancer battling challenges, I've evolved my career and life's work into a Professional Empowerment Coach who's affectionately become labeled a Resilience Expert. It's funny how we have to go through the fires of life and come out the other end to have people want to hear what we have to say.

I'll be the first one to tell anybody that if I didn't get sick with cancer, I would've remained on my life's path of being a Physical Therapist & Clinic Owner and I would've NEVER created the ThePositiveDrip.com[5] blog. Perhaps it's true what they say –

"Life happens FOR you, instead of to you."

You may not agree with me and my mental imagery and visualization techniques, and yes, I'm not an expert in this psycho-motor field of science, but I'm gratefully still here, completely alive, and I've recently put a checkmark beside one of the things on my bucket list - I have achieved the freedom of walking completely on my own on January 3rd, 2021.

Friends and family are now happily asking me what's next for me and I aloofly reply - "whatever my mind can think up".

Perhaps my next goal and my next metaphorical mountain to climb will be to trot, jog, run, and / or sprint once again by December 31, 2021. After almost being ushered off of this planet, the greatest life lesson that I learned, and I'd love to share with you is:

---

5. http://www.ThePositiveDrip.com

While living in the 5 different hospitals in 2016 & 2017 surrounded by death and sickness 24/7. My travelling soul had come to the sky opening realization that the biggest lie that we've ALL been led to believe, me included, is that we all have "Time" and a long list of "Some days" and an unlimited amount of "I'll Do It Later" opportunities. Truth is, that's completely false.

Nobody knows that day or the hour of one's last breath. My spiritual and visual journeys, which allowed me to roam beyond the four walls of those hospitals, had taught me how extremely important it is to live in the "NOW" and to get rid of life's many "distractions", which we are all too guilty of having, in order to clearly chase down as many of your personal check marks as possible so that way when you do pass away you can "Die Empty" bringing no unfinished earthly business with you to the grave.

My friends, Your Imagination, Mental Imagery, and Affirmed Visualizations are the preview of your life's coming attractions. Everything ever created in this lifetime, and on this planet is born twice. Once in the mind, and then once in the world. Protect your goals, dreams, and visions and surround yourself with people at your ambition level or above. We only "Get" one chance at life folks, this 'aint no dress rehearsal.

Ladies & Gentlemen, I'm the Proud Son of the late great Mr. Gregorio Hierco Beltijar - (a Man of humble beginnings, who weathered every single storm that life threw at him, and was living proof that Dreams CAN come True) - Because of him, and my loving mother, I'm a believer in people, I'm a foolish dreamer, with my head forever in the clouds, whose thoughts have taken me to places where logic doesn't exist on route to returning and claiming victory over the Greatest Adversities of my life. Being a believer in the power of visualization gives me the trusting ability to see people, or anything, for what they can become and not necessarily for where they're currently at.

If you're looking to get to that next level of personal achievement but don't know how to get there, I invite you to reach out to me at ThePositiveDrip.com[6] and together we'll conquer your mountains of perceived cant's and paralyzing impossibilities as we chase your best and seek the greatest version of Yourselves. Know that I'm Looking forward to speaking with you - "Tomorrow" ☺

Sincerely,

Nelson Beltijar www.ThePositiveDrip.com[7]

Empowerment Coach • Speaker • Author

---

6. http://www.ThePositiveDrip.com

7. https://d.docs.live.net/4927f85f42ada7cc/Documents/www.ThePositiveDrip.com

Face Your Goliath

By Chucky Smiley

Do you possess the mental fortitude to overcome any adversity? Do you have the courage to face the Goliath standing in front of you? If the answer is no, let me share with you two principles that enabled a teenage shepherd boy to defeat a seasoned warrior who had years of combat experience.

Surprisingly, these two principles are love and the ability to devise a strategy. We all have giants we must face and if you're not eager or willing to face this trail, I believe this short story will aid you in overcoming this adversity.

David vs Goliath

In the biblical story, David versus Goliath we meet a teenage shepherd by the name of David from the nation of Israel. Unbeknownst to this young man his life is tied to an encounter with a mighty Philistine warrior from Gath who stood nearly seven feet tall. This encounter is actually a battle between two men representing their respective countries. In an effort to prevent an all-out war, the giant from Gath, Goliath proposes a challenge.

He challenges the nation of Israel to nominate a warrior to battle the giant. The terms of the battle are simple; the loser will become slaves to the winner. Once the King and soldiers of Israel heard this plea, they were terrified and for forty days no one came forth to fight the giant, until the young shepherd boy heard the taunts of Goliath that echoed through the valley of Elah.

Was the young man crazy? Was he willing to risk life for fame? Or was he just thinking about the riches he might receive if he were able to defeat this giant from Gath. The reason David desired to fight Goliath was much deeper than the superficial, aforementioned questions.

Love

Albert Einstein the German-born theoretical physicist and Nobel prize winner in Physics, who also developed the theory of relativity and is known for his influence on the philosophy of science is credited with leaving a powerful message about love to his daughter. This beautiful letter details how love is the strongest force in the world. Below you will find an excerpt from this letter:

"There is an extremely powerful force that, so far, science has not found a formal explanation to. It is a force that includes and governs all others and is even behind any phenomenon operating in the universe and has not yet been identified by us."

This universal force is LOVE.

When scientists looked for a unified theory of the universe, they forgot the most powerful unseen force.

Love is Light that enlightens those who give and receive it.

Love is gravity, because it makes some people feel attracted to others.

Love is power, because it multiplies the best we have and allows humanity not to be extinguished in their blind selfishness. Love unfolds and reveals.

For love we live and die.

Love is God and God is Love.

This force explains everything and gives meaning to life. This is the variable that we have ignored for too long, maybe because we are afraid of love because it is the only energy in the universe that man has not learned to drive at will.

To give visibility to love, I made a simple substitution in my most famous equation:

If instead of $E = mc^2$, we accept that the energy to heal the world can be obtained through love, multiplied by the speed of light squared, we arrive at the conclusion that love is the most powerful force there is, because it has no limits.

Like Albert Einstein, David was also motivated by love and this love gave him the courage to stand against the giant, Goliath. Furthermore, David's love for his God, family, and country was the reason why he was willing to risk his family name and more importantly his own life. His love is also shown by his obedience to his Father. The reason David came to the Valley of Elah on that fateful day, is because his Father asked him to bring his brothers some food.

At this time, his brothers were soldiers in the King's army and manning the battlefield. As previously mentioned, the motivation to face a giant stemmed from the love David had in his heart. The evidence for this profound statement about David can be found a few years earlier when David was anointed by the prophet Samuel to be the next king of Israel. Keep in mind, David was chosen after Samuel examined each of his eight brothers. This moment in David's young life confirmed what he already knew and that was God loved him and God was going to use him in miraculous ways. David's faith grew tremendously from this and so did his love for his God, family, and country.

Strategy

How did a shepherd boy beat a seasoned warrior? The answer is quite simple. David had a better game plan or for those familiar with military terms, strategy.

David never intended to go toe to toe with the larger, more experienced Goliath. We know this to be true because he rejects the heavy armor that King Saul offered to David.

David's strategy was to use his talent that was developed and honed through years of protecting his father's sheep. This skill was the art of using a slingshot. David was so good at using his slingshot that he was able to kill a bear and a lion. He clearly was a professional sharpshooter with this sling in his hand. Researchers believe the force David was able to throw a stone was comparable to the force of a .45 caliber handgun. Additionally, David knew his best shot of defeating Goliath was to expose his weakness. If you're familiar with the story, Goliath is covered head to toe in armor so what is his weakness? His weakness is that his forehead is exposed and due to the weight of the armour Goliath is slow and lethargic.

David places a well aimed stone right between the eyes of Goliath and he falls flat on his face. While Goliath is momentarily incapacitated, David runs up to Goliath, pulls out his sword, and cuts his head off.

In life, we all will have to face challenges and endure storms that arise. This is a guarantee. The good news is, if we are strong mentally, we will be able to endure these difficult times.

In the Bible, Jesus knew tough times were soon to come for his disciples so he told them *"I have told you these things, so that in me you may have peace. In this world you will have trouble. But take heart! I have overcome the world."* The reason Jesus told them this before it happened was to prepare them and more importantly to encourage them, so they wouldn't lose hope.

Some lucky people will use the unfortunate hand they've been dealt as fuel to help them reach their destiny. If these same lucky people are able to endure these undesirable circumstances and not throw in the towel, they will realize the true power that is inside of them. And the power revealed in them will propel them forward in life because they will be able to overcome any other storm they may encounter.

American President, Theodore Roosevelt once said, *"Nothing in the world is worth having or worth doing unless it means effort, pain, difficulty...I have never in my life envied a human being who led an easy life. I have envied a great many people who led difficult lives and led them well."*

Your success in life is directly tied to how you're able to respond to the obstacles you encounter.

These obstacles could be the lack of resources when starting a business, the heavy workload of completing a degree from a higher learning institution, or maybe even raising a child by yourself with very little help from the other parent or other family members.

Take notes, to persevere in life we must find the inner willpower to stay in the fight, follow through, and exert maximum effort until the end to achieve our goals, dreams, and visions. Finally, we also need a game plan that will help us to strategically plot our courses of action. This gameplan will make the vision plan to you and your team.

Like David, God has given all of us a specific mission we're supposed to complete while on this earth. In order to accomplish this mission, we must develop mental toughness and we have to find a way to persevere against difficult times and anything else that may come our way. Quitting is not a possibility. If you need a break, take it, but once the break is over get back to it. Find the thing you love the most and use it as motivation to help you continue the fight. Lastly, it's essential that we devise a strategy to assist us in accomplishing our dreams just like David did when he destroyed Goliath. This plan will serve as a roadmap and will help you to navigate uncharted territory. Lastly, we must remember anything worth having is worth fighting for.

Well-Armed to Win

By Aaron Gryder

Success takes guts, I was sixteen years old, weighed eighty-seven pounds and didn't speak Spanish. I was in Mexico to start my career. I told a trainer if I could ride his filly in a race, we'd win.

"Why would I put you on my best horse? He asked. "You've never even won a race. I've got a slow horse you can ride to get some experience". That was all the opportunity I needed. It was only my eighteenth race to ride. Running down the stretch we were behind several horses, but I kept pushing. With only a few strides left, we angled to the outside racing towards the lead. At the wire.... It was too close to call. Three horses crossed the finish line together. The judges posted Ragen Henry, the horse I was riding, the winner by a nose. I had won my first race. The next week, I rode his filly, and we did win.

I have always loved horse racing. And I believe that if you find something you truly love, follow your passion and you will always win in the end!

I was born into a loving family in Southern California in 1970. My father owned a small business, and my mother took good care of my brother and me. We enjoyed riding our bikes and playing with our friends. My father had a great work ethic, but, when his business went bankrupt, we lost our house. Dad's small office became our home.

At that point, he started his gardening business, worked from sunrise to sunset to provide for our family and Mom took on work at a department store. On the day I saw my parents empty a tall wooden bank full of change to pay bills, I realized the struggles they felt. Although I must have known intuitively that they struggled, they always told us that everything was okay. In spite of our financial struggles, my parents were full of love and it radiated throughout our home. One of my proudest childhood moments was putting $50 that I earned under their pillow.

During the summers, I would visit Santa Anita racetrack with my grandparents. They were big horse racing fans and went to the track often. The horses both scared and fascinated me. I was amazed by their power, beauty, size, and speed. I loved to hear their hooves skipping across the dirt as they raced by.

At four years old, I declared that I wanted to be a jockey. I imagined racing down the stretch and WINNING!

My desire to become a jockey continued to grow. Many people supported my dreams, but others doubted them. Some thought I'd be too big or wouldn't be strong enough. They asked, how could I be a jockey if I was afraid of horses?

An extraordinary opportunity came my way when I met Rudy Campas, a retired jockey.

I shared my heart's desire, and he invited me to stay at his farm the following summer to

learn to care for horses. I was so excited; I couldn't focus on school and my grades slipped. All I could think about was racing. After ninth grade, I accepted Rudy's offer.

On the farm, I awoke before sunrise to feed and groom the horses and clean their stalls. One day, Rudy told me to saddle a horse and get on. I was nervous, but very excited. After riding for twenty minutes, however, Rudy said, "Kid, you're a natural." I didn't know what I had done right, but the fear of falling had kept me on. I then realized I could create positive results by facing my fears. Each day, as I rode, I gained confidence. My understanding of horses developed, and I became a horseman. I worked hard and didn't want to lose momentum. My parents understood that I'd gotten the opportunity of a lifetime and allowed me to stay on Rudy's farm.

I quit school to focus on my dream and I was in heaven. One day, while at the track, a gentleman approached me and asked if I'd try out for a Del Monte Juice advertisement.

My grandfather took me to Hollywood for the audition; I got the role of a jockey. I made enough money from that commercial to eventually buy my first car and all my racing equipment.

At sixteen, I was licensed to gallop at the track. Rudy picked a horse he knew I could handle. The first lap around the track went smoothly, but then the stirrup broke, and I fell.

My foot was caught in the saddle, and I was dragged for thirty yards before shaking loose. The horse ran back to the barn, playfully kicking and bucking. Physically, I was fine, but my ego was bruised. Immediately a racing official trotted over to ask, "Son, do

you have a license?" I proudly answered, "Yes ma'am" and handed it over. She galloped off. As I walked back to the barn, I heard, "Aaron Gryder, see the stewards" being amplified over the loudspeaker. Not knowing I was in trouble, I asked Rudy, "What are stewards?" His reply wasn't comforting: "It's not good," he answered.

The stewards ruled me off that day, saying I was not ready to work on the racetrack.

I had worked years to get this chance and I failed. I was devastated. As Rudy drove us home, he encouraged me not to give up. "Don't worry about it," he said. I wiped my tears with the back of my hand and looked out the window, reflecting on my recent embarrassment. I was not giving up!

I continued working towards my goal with tunnel vision. Within six months, I was a licensed jockey. I started racing at Caliente Racetrack in Tijuana, Mexico. There, I gained confidence as I honed my skills. The horses ran well, and I was winning daily. I needed this experience because I was moving to the most elite racetrack in the country, Santa Anita Park. When I arrived, top trainers gave me opportunities to ride their horses. I was now riding against the best jockeys in the world. I observed and learned from each of them. Jockeys don't have coaches, so I had to figure out how to become great!

My parents returned to southern California to watch me race. They were my biggest fans. My father regularly came to the track after work to watch me ride. One morning, before leaving town for a couple days, he gave me a big hug and said "I love you, Son. Go win a race for me tomorrow." I didn't know that would be the last time I'd see him. That night, the police woke me to give the sad news: While driving, Dad had a heart attack and went off the side of a mountain. He was 42 years old. In an instant, I went from being a 17-year-old kid, to becoming a man. I decided I would take on his responsibilities and provide for our family.

The next day I went to ride. Some thought I shouldn't, but I knew I must when I recalled

my father's final words to me. "I love you son, go win a race for me tomorrow." It was pouring rain and the track was muddy. I rode a small filly named Tom's Sweety; she had

never won a race. She jumped from the gate slowly and was trailing early. I could hardly

see with all the mud flying, but as the race progressed, she advanced. We navigated through traffic. With a 1/4 of a mile to go, we were three lengths behind the leaders. She

had momentum, and I knew we were going to win. I was crying as we crossed the finish

line first. We did it; I won a race for my dad!

Throughout my life I have used the loss of, and lessons learned from, my father for inspiration. One month after he died, I became the first, and only apprentice to ever lead

the jockey standings at Hollywood Park racetrack. Since then, I have travelled the world

and won prestigious races. Horse racing is the Sport of Kings, and I have ridden winners for sheiks, princes, kings, and queens.

In 2008 though, I struggled to win races. I continued asking trainers to ride their horses. One morning, I stood next to a trainer watching his horse gallop. The horse hadn't competed for over a year and a half due to an injury. I asked if I could get on him, the trainer said, "No". He thought the horse was too aggressive and wasn't ready to run fast. I confidently said, "If he doesn't relax for me, I'll never ask again."

He reluctantly agreed. His name was Well Armed, and we got along well. He improved daily. That year, he won a few big races before being invited to compete in the 2009 Dubai World Cup with prize money of $6,000,000. Not only did Well Armed compete, he dominated, winning by 14 lengths.

In one of the lowest points of my career, I was able to find a horse that would win the biggest race in the world.

As a youngster, I feared horses, dropped out of school, and left home at 13 years old to

become a jockey. I had a dream, and I believed in myself. I didn't know the exact steps

to success. I just knew I was willing to take that first step and commit to the hard work.

Like Well Armed when the odds were against him, he concentrated on getting better and was confident in himself. He proved his doubters wrong by becoming the best in the world. In my career, I have won over 4,000 races worldwide, I have also lost 26,000. If you quit on your dreams because you encounter losses, you will always find excuses and shortcomings. Learn from your losses, be dedicated, persistent, and relentless. Don't ever give up! When you find your passion, you will discover how to win. Live Your Dreams!

How Losing my Job Helped me Find my Life

By Katie Corbett

Within eighteen months of graduating from college, I had moved four times, paid off a huge chunk of my student loan debt, and found and lost my first full-time job. The following three years brought little change on the surface, but I learned so much about myself and what I wanted. I also learned how to overcome the greatest challenge yet – defeating the monster in my brain: anxiety.

In this quick story, I'm going to reveal a tool I come back to again and again to overcome anxiety. My hope is that you will be able to use some of these techniques, too. My journey began as I was telling a friend about how I had been unjustly fired from that full-time job. As we sat in her car, her dad driving up in front, I told the story about how toxic my boss had been, how little my coworkers had done to support me, and how I was working odd jobs to make ends meet now. What surprised me the most, I told my friend, were the lasting after-effects of that experience.

"Now, whenever anyone says they want to talk with me, I feel this sense of dread in my stomach," I explained. "I keep being afraid they're going to scream at me the way my former boss did. She totally wrecked my reputation at that company and used things I said out of context."

"I had a similar experience," her dad piped up.

He told me his story of how he had been accused of things he didn't do and been professionally dragged through the mud.

"How did you get over it?" I asked. "What did you do to get better?"

"Honestly, Katie, I'm still not over it," he said. "It's been years."

I made the decision then and there that this would not be me. I made the choice to "get over it," no matter what I had to do.

I recalled a party a year earlier, where I'd been talking with this random guy about psychology. He mentioned Neuro-Linguistic Programming (NLP for short), a practice where, as he put it, "I can learn to read the behavior of others and adapt my communication style to get them to do what I want."

I had gotten a book on the topic because, while I wasn't big on the idea of mind-control, I knew negotiation wasn't my strong suit. I figured any advice I could get would help. As I'd flipped through the book, I'd noticed sections on reframing experiences, healing trauma, and overcoming anxiety. I thought, "That's cool," and then put the book away.

As I began the journey to address my anxiety around my horrible experiences from the job, I recalled some of the concepts in that book and pulled it out for another look. When I wasn't working on one-of contract projects, hanging out with friends, or volunteering at my church, I stretched out on my bed and applied some of the techniques I read about in the NLP book.

I mentally brought myself back to the times my boss had screamed at me and changed her voice in my head to sound like Mickey Mouse or Donald Duck. This made me laugh to myself. I mentally turned down the volume of her voice in my memory, so I could more clearly recall the words she said and realize they were not true. I pictured myself facing away from her and got to the point to where I could picture myself getting up and walking out of the room. I pictured some of my good friends sitting there with me, telling me that I didn't need to listen to that kind of talk and telling me that I could leave. After hours spent applying NLP techniques, the memories no longer had a stinging quality, and my anxiety around the whole experience began to fade.

I initiated working on addressing anxiety triggers that stemmed from that experience. When someone said they wanted to talk, I started asking what they wanted to talk about so that I would know the basic content of the discussion. I began paying attention to my bodily signals, particularly when my stomach was queasy or my heartbeat raced, so I could remove myself from uncomfortable conversations, or neutralize situations before they could get out-of-hand. I learned what to say to set boundaries and call people out on behavior. I gave myself permission to leave the room, hang up the phone, or take a break when conversations started to feel uncomfortable.

My brain was on its way to healing, but I was still feeling deep shame about having lost that job, or for not quitting sooner, or even for not seeing the signs that it was a toxic environment in the first place. With the help of the NLP book and some good, supportive friends, I worked on reframing my experience and overcoming the anxiety that arose from the memories and experiences.

The NLP book also had information about how to plan for future outcomes, so I began to apply that advice. I thought about the lessons I'd learned about the kinds of people I wanted to work with, and the qualities I wanted in my next boss. I thought a lot about what I wanted in terms of work hours, company size, and work environment. I thought back on my favorite jobs, and the times in my life when I'd felt most fulfilled. I evaluated the takeaways I got from that first full-time work experience, both positive and negative.

I learned that I wanted to work on a smaller team with people who would each pull their weight and hold themselves accountable. I wanted a boss who was honest, and who appreciated my honest feedback.

I realized that I never wanted to work full-time in a cubicle again. I learned that I thrive working remotely and, in a culture where I can set my own hours. I thrive in settings with project-based work, rather than work that comes in unpredictable chunks, such as customer service.

That first full-time job taught me that I can be productive, even when experiencing negative situations where I'm being actively criticized. I learned that I could manage my emotional responses, even in environments when others were not managing theirs. I learned that I am a person who trusts others, is transparent and honest, and thinks the best of people. While each of these qualities likely contributed to my acceptance of the way I was treated in that job, I have done my best to put myself in work environments where those qualities are appreciated, rather than used as leverage for someone to push me around. Most importantly, that job led me, however indirectly, to NLP. I have come back to this powerful tool time and again; there is so much to learn about how the brain works and how our thoughts and feelings impact us.

Conquering the monster of anxiety is still a work-in-progress. I'm still establishing and enforcing boundaries around how I spend my time and how others treat me, and I'm paying attention to and respecting my body's stress response signals.

If you, too, discover that anxiety is part of your experience of life on this planet, I encourage you to take these tools and apply them to initiate overcoming it. If you were in a situation where someone undermined your work, screamed at you, or told you that you are worthless and that you couldn't do the job, you didn't deserve to be treated like that. If someone treated you kindly one day and yelled at you the next, you didn't deserve it. If someone's emotional responses are impacting you so much that you forget to shower for a week, or if exhaustion from your job is making you sick, giving you stomach, shoulder or back pain, or making it impossible to relax when you're off work, you don't deserve that.

NLP is a powerful tool that can help you heal from those experiences and overcome the anxiety that lingers. I'm living proof that healing and triumph are possible.

——————-

Katie Corbett is a writer specializing in customer success stories. She works with companies to tell the stories of their happy customers through customer case studies, impactful testimonials, and inspiring reviews. Connect with Katie on LinkedIn at Linkedin.com/in/katie-m-corbett/

Fiction Turned Real Life

By Michelle Hardy

Many years ago, I was going through a tumultuous time where I was struggling emotionally and financially, but what I realized is that I was able to use my power of visualization to turn my fictional writing into a reality. Whatever you write about can come true, what you think about will manifest and what you focus on will become reality.

Years prior I had written a fictional short story which delves into an intimate relationship between a little girl and an elderly woman with an emphasis on giving. I had always written poetry but nothing like this story. The story just kind of sat in my repertoire of writing but I wasn't sharing it.

One particular Christmas, I had no money to buy presents for family or friends. I was in a very depressed state of mind. I had always perused thrift stores and one day while driving I happened to see a new thrift store that I hadn't been in before, so I quickly jotted inside. I was perusing the aisles, but nothing stood out to me and as I started to leave the store, I looked over at the checkout and behind the glass counter, I noticed a huge punch bowl and 13 teacups with gold trim on the top rim and the bottom as well. The serving set was so beautiful. Turns out these were the same cups I had written about in my fictional short story years before, and here they were, staring me right in the face.

I asked the lady at the checkout counter how much the entire set was. It was just the amount of money I had. I purchased the bowl with the cups, wrapped them as gifts and gave the fictional short story with the cups to my family and friends; they all loved it.

As the years went by, I met people along my journey and daily I would share the story and a gift from the story. I would walk around town with a satchel filled with 'Random Acts of Kindness'; passing out kindness wherever the opportunity presented itself. For many years I have been sharing the story and kindness.

One day I was in my office and the phone rang. It was a woman who used to be a customer. She said, "*I don't know if you remember me but you gave me a gift with a beautiful story.*" I instantly knew who she was. I distinctly remember this customer because she walked with a certain hunch in her back, bent over, not being able to stand straight and would address you in the down position while turning her head upwards. One of the sweetest ladies you'll ever meet.

My conversation with the woman on the phone continued, she said "It's so wonderful that you give out such a beautiful story and give away the things that the elderly woman gave to you." I paused but didn't bother to correct her; however, it made me think. I questioned myself, "Michelle was there a 'real' lady like the elderly woman in your story?" Oh My GOD! There was a lady!

Not even realizing it while on this journey, I had not related the elderly woman in my fictional story to a real person in my own life. I did have a 'real' elderly woman I had met on my journey.

I started thinking about the things I had written about in my story and the things me and the "real" elderly lady had done together. I thought, was it all coming true? Was what I had written as fictional, manifesting itself?

In my fictional story the elderly woman had given the little girl treasures like priceless silver, valuable jewelry and things from her own childhood. The 'real' elderly woman in my own life had given me those same things. In my fictional short story, the elderly woman died. In my own personal life, the "real" elderly woman died as well. The same way I had written about the death in my book is the same way it happened to me.

There were so many correlations to my fictional story and my personal life, it was like I had written my fate. The customer had to bring it to my attention on my journey of doing Random Acts of Kindness that my fictional story was coming true in my own life. What you think about can literally manifest itself in your own life and in my case without my even knowing it.

As time passed, someone suggested I write a full complete book. At first, I was reluctant because I thought, "what else can I write about?" It dawned on me that I could just write about my own personal life and the experiences I actually had because now it would be synonymous with the fictional now true short story.

I continue to share the story by speaking to teens and adults about giving. As what is given to me, I share with whomever crosses my path. I share the story and something from the story. I will continue this journey as my purpose in life is to give without ceasing as the elderly woman had given to me. I am always honored to share what it's like to give in beautiful ways. This journey has taken me on a quest to not only give without ceasing but teach everyone in the world how to give instantly, right where they are. It really costs nothing to give. Give love, give time, give joy. To make a huge impact on students' lives I help them gain confidence in their giving to make an ultimate impact with what they have at their fingertips. The student will be able to clearly articulate their own personal message of giving by their actions.... Even for the shyest person. The tools I leave with students are adaptable to their current situation. I teach about how they can give with more passion, authenticity and empathy. Always remember to focus on what is important and it will come true for you as it did for me.

I admit my book is designed with students in mind. I welcome you to read the first two chapters[8] of my book 'Mrs. Eels Basement of Beautiful Magical Things' at michellehardy.org/thestory[9] and to purchase the book at the same site. There are an array of questions and a small glossary in the back of the book to assist educators with delving into what it is like to be kind. A lot of times people are stumped and run out of ways to show kindness, but I see kindness in everything we do, everyday we live. It's a matter of opening the mind up to possibilities. Be yourself in your giving and you can never go wrong.

If I can take a fictional story and focus on giving and turn it into a movement as my life's work, just think about what you can do. Go forth and do good in the world.

---

8. https://bekindco.wixsite.com/mrseelsbasement/book

9. https://michellehardy.org/thestory

Michelle Tamiko Hardy

Oakland, CA

Author, Philanthropist, Inspirational Speaker

(415) 378-3681

mmtamikohardy@gmail.com

Website: michellehardy.org/thestory[10]

Social Media Pages:

facebook.com/thegivingguru[11]

instagram.com/michelletamikohardy[12]

twitter.com/mtamikohardy[13]

---

10. https://michellehardy.org/thestory
11. https://facebook.com/thegivingguru
12. https://instagram.com/michelletamikohardy
13. https://twitter.com/mtamikohardy

A Quest to Find Purpose

By Beenie Mann

We all have a purpose. Some big, some smaller. Some fulfill their purpose while others do not.

Often, I wonder how many people know their path and purpose from the beginning? I certainly had no clue!

Growing up was rough. There was a lot of physical and mental abuse. Clearly, no role-models to emulate. No footsteps to follow. At least none I was interested in, or that would lead me to a better life...

There was no direction. The only direction, if I would have carried on the family tradition, was a dead end. No one to turn to for guidance out of the hole. No one to give me hope or encouragement. Nothing but the dream of a better life.

Yes, there were classmates who seemed to have it all. I never fit in and was constantly made fun of. How did they get so lucky to seemingly have it all? What is wrong with me? Am I doomed to be stuck where I am?

Fortunately, I was able to go to a private, boarding school in Germany. Granted, I was a ward of the state, but I did not care. For the first time in my life, I felt safe. For the first time, I allowed myself to have hope for a better outcome, a better future. There, I was shown different POSSIBILITIES! For the first time, I was given a lifeline.

There, I developed a hunger for more. There, the seed for a better life was planted. There, for the first time, I learned that I was not worthless. There, I learned that I deserve a better life. For the first time, I was shown that I was worth it and deserving. Being there, were the best 5 years of my youth and young adulthood.

I did not realize it at that time as the self-doubt, low self-esteem, and insecurities ran very deep. However, the seed was planted! It was buried deep, but it was there. It was the seed of hope, desire, and the knowledge that anything is possible.

The same year I had graduated from my school, I met this very handsome and nice soldier. We met the 'old-fashioned way'... drunk in a bar (I like to toss that tidbit in as it was over 30 years ago that we met, and we are still very happily married).

He was a soldier in the U.S. Army, and he stole my heart. I knew I would follow him to the end of the world! A few (3) months later we were engaged and two months after that, we were married. Looking back, I am still in awe.

Anyway, here I am, a military spouse. No idea what that meant at the time. All I knew was that I am in love, and everything will work out... Somehow, it always does!

At the time I was working to make ends meet but I knew that was not my calling. It was something I simply had to do to survive and while working odd jobs, I always wondered what else I could do. How could I better myself and our circumstances? How can I nourish that seed?

Military life is not for the faint of heart. We have to deal with deployments, extended field (training) exercises, just to name a few. As the spouse that stays behind, we have to make sure all is running smoothly, raise the kids, help the other spouses, be there for our service member... in short, keep it all together and running so our servicemember can focus 100% on their job and not worry about things at home.

If I had to live my life over, I would do it all again!!!

Once we had children, we both agreed for me to stay home and raise them. Since I was a 'latchkey' child growing up, I swore I would always be there for my own kids. Now I am a military spouse and a mom. That was my identity. My purpose.

So I thought and kept telling myself. Yet, there was this internal hunger to do something to contribute to our financial well-being. During that time, I was introduced to network marketing. It was alluring to me as it could be a vehicle to earn some income while being my own boss. It would allow me to be home with our kids, raising them, yet help pay the bills.

It was easy getting started as we lived in the US at that time. Once we were back in Germany, it was impossible to continue due to the SoFA (Status of Forces) agreement between the US and Germany. It was a blow to my still fragile mindset. Now what? The seed that was starting to take root hit a dry spell.

While stationed in Germany, not able to earn an income, I became active within the Family Readiness Group (FRG) of our unit and the post overall. Army Community Service (ACS) offered a variety of classes for spouses and best of all... they offered FREE childcare while we take the classes!!! Sign me up!!!

What I loved about the classes was that they were not only subject specific (FRG, money, etc.), they also had elements of personal development. Something I was introduced to via the network marketing company but never delved into. I wanted to learn more! So much so, that I received my certificate as an Army Family Team Building Master Trainer. Teaching other spouses and help them navigate through military life was nourishment for my little seed.

Once back in the States, I went back to network marketing. Signed up with one company, switched to another, and another, and another. Although I loved the products and the training, it was not for me, and I invested way more money than I earned. I like to compare that time with the gardener who is looking for the perfect fertilizer to grow their garden.

With the kids being old enough, I ventured back into the workforce. It did not last long for I had developed a thirst and hunger for being my own boss. In my heart I have known for a long time that I was an entrepreneur. I just did not know what that would look like or where that would lead me.

Here I was bouncing from one thing to another working on figuring out my purpose. One MLM, job, opportunity, after the other. From the outside looking in, it appeared that I was flighty and could not finish or stick to anything I started. To me, I found all the things I did not like and did not want to do. It was a matter of perspective.

Finally, on 1 April 2018, at age 52, a thought that changed everything! In that moment I decided to do on purpose and with purpose what I have been doing my whole life! Help people smile, be better, be more, and see different perspectives. Turns out, I have been a coach/mentor my whole life. YEAH!! I finally found my purpose! The seed started to turn into a plant!!!

While working on figuring out how to move forward as a coach, strangers kept asking me about my book. Or asked if I had written one. WHAT???

There was a time, where I felt I had to share my story. However, that was so far out of my realm of anything that I never paid much attention to it. Maybe I would be a public speaker sharing my story and inspire others not to give up. Some day. But a book???...

Here I was being nudged by the Universe about MY book that was not even on my radar by a long shot.

Certainly, I have enough experiences to share and fill a few books. Experiences to inspire and help so many people around the world.

Since I rarely back down from a challenge I said: Fine! You want me to write this book... Give it to me!

Well, you know what they say... Ask and you shall receive!

Receive I did! Apparently, it was time for my story to be told and the lessons I learned to be shared. My first book, Happiness Matters – Unleash Your Superpower in 7 Easy Steps, was written and published in under 3 months! From there, I started a YouTube channel where I interviewed guests. Our local TV station had me on as a regular for almost a year. Public speaking had become a reality. And so much more...

There are many more books inside of me that are waiting to come to life. The seed that was planted so long ago has turned into a beautiful flower.

It does not matter how long it takes or how many detours we must take to find our purpose. What matters is that we never give up and continue growing. There is so much fun in the journey if we let it flow. It is not going to be a straight line. There will be set-backs, twists, and turns and that is alright. The growth we get to experience as a person is worth every step, every tear, and every pearl of sweat. This is something nobody will ever be able to take away from you.

Listen to and follow your heart. Most of all... KEEP GOING!

If a German girl, who grew up in an abusive environment can do it, you can do it too!

To receive your complimentary Quick Guide to Happiness, email

info@mattersofperspective.com (Subject: Quick Guide)

Follow my author page: amzn.to/2Pb2I9m[14]

---

14. https://amzn.to/2Pb2I9m

Your Journey Has Purpose - Do What You Love

By Luis Sandoval

Have you ever asked yourself one of the following questions at one time or another? What is my purpose here on Earth? What is my calling? What career path should I take? Will I ever accomplish my dreams? Can I pursue my passion and get paid well for it? I have asked these questions numerous times in my life. Well, I am here to tell you, based on my personal experiences, that you can find your passion, and that dreams do come true.

The path to my dream job is not like other stories you have heard about, stories of people who go to college, get a degree and go straight into their dream career of choice. It took me about six years to find my passion, and ten years to land my dream job. Now, I'm finally doing what I love and getting paid for it.

As I look back at my life, I can now see that my journey had a purpose. Every job I had served a purpose, and it paved the way to my dream job. Even the jobs that became drudgery served a purpose. Without those jobs, I wouldn't be where I am today.

One summer, when I was in my late teens, I got a job as a sales assistant in a car dealership. It was not the best experience for me, but I acquired a lot of knowledge while working there. I also knew that there was a reason for me being on that job, so I stayed there, worked hard, and learned. At the age of twenty-one, I got involved in the media department at my church. That department was short-staffed and in need of volunteers. I had no prior experience, but in my heart, I wanted to serve, so I offered to help. Someone in the department trained me, and after a while, I started liking it. In fact, I developed a passion for audiovisual, and the passion grew stronger every day. I knew then that I had found something special. Little did I know that my journey had a purpose.

I continued to volunteer at the church while working. One day while I was setting up the sound system in the auditorium of the church, I said to myself, *I would love to do this for a living and get paid for it*. That's when I realized that working in the audiovisual industry was my calling. However, I continued to bounce from job to job working at a hotel, delivering medical supplies, and driving celebrities around. None of those worked out for me. One month before my wedding day, I became unemployed. That was not a good way to start a marriage, I knew. Little did I know that my journey had a purpose.

Three weeks before my wedding, I received a call from a recruiter requesting an interview. I honestly didn't want another sales job; but there I was, a few weeks away from my wedding, so I couldn't say no. Needless to say, I took the job, and I was so glad that I did. When I tell you that I loved that job, believe me! Oh, how I loved it! It had some great perks. The health insurance package was amazing and the time for my shift was perfect. The work was easy, and the salary was decent. It was great for the first few years, but as we all know, sometimes, good things come to an end.

As much as I loved that job, it started to become drudgery. I lost all the excitement I had and instead of gratitude, I felt anguish on the days that I had to work. I felt like I had no purpose being there. I knew that there was more to me than being a salesperson. Over time, I started to resent my job.

In the meantime, my passion for audiovisual kept burning inside me. I knew that audiovisual gave me that sense of fulfillment. One day I remembered thinking to myself, *I would love to do audiovisual and get paid for it*. Suddenly, a light bulb came on, and it was then, that I decided to act and make my desire, my reality. I began talking with several people I knew who worked in the audiovisual industry, about opportunities to work with them, or in their field. Nothing happened at first, but I kept asking. I was persistent. I kept telling them my story and letting them know my desire to make my volunteer job, my career. Meanwhile, I kept working on the job that was causing me distress, because I had bills to pay. It also crossed my mind, that if I had a different position in the company, and made more money, that would provide me some satisfaction. I applied for other jobs in the organization, but it seemed as if God had closed the doors on those opportunities for me on purpose. I grew frustrated.

Eventually, after nine years on that burdensome job, God set me free. I was let go right before the holidays. Great timing, right? Well, all things, good or bad, happen for a reason. Little did I know that this part of my journey had a purpose. I was unemployed for five months when a fellow worshiper from my church, who worked in the audiovisual industry called me and said, "Hey Lu, I went for an interview, and they didn't choose me for the position. Here is their number. Call them and see what happens." So, I called, then emailed them my resume. Within a few days, I got a call back for an interview.

During the meeting, the interviewer sensed my interest and became adamant about me getting into the company. He said "I have this position for you, but I also want you to get interviewed for the corporate position that is available. I see that you don't have corporate experience but I'm going to send you to be interviewed for this position anyway. If it doesn't work out, then, come back to me." It seemed as if God told him to give me a job, one way or another. I could not believe what I was hearing!

The interview process was long. After each interview, I waited for a response, and then I was asked to come back in to meet someone else. I was told that the company was looking at many qualified individuals with degrees from all kinds of great schools and backgrounds. The interesting thing about this interview was that they kept calling me back to meet each top-tier level executive in the company. One of the executives explained that, even though I didn't have the degree that was required for the position, both my experience with audiovisual and customer service made me stand out significantly. They considered my years of commitment to both, and they hired me!

I ended up getting my dream job at the age of thirty-four. How awesome is that!

The crazy part of this to me is that I wasn't even looking for a corporate position, and I had no college degrees or certifications, which a position like the one I got required. What I had was a job that made me uncomfortable, and a volunteer job that gave me so much sense of pride and joy. I kept working at both jobs, even though I had different feelings about each. With stick-to-itiveness, I held on to them both, and it paid off.

Fast forward: eight years later, and here I am, working for one of the top three social media companies in the world. The learning opportunities are great, and I have the potential to continue to grow in the company. The awesome thing is that I'm doing what I love to do and getting paid for it. The best part is, I don't even consider it work. I no longer hate Mondays but look forward to them because I get to do what I love.

When you are called to do something, just do your part, and let your Creator do the rest. He puts those gifts, talents, and dreams inside of you. Your job is to use those talents and gifts to serve others and help them make their lives better. Don't let your talents and gifts go to waste. Even if you are only a volunteer, use your talents and gifts to be of help to others.

When trying to find your career path or your calling, life has a way of giving you clues to your passion and purpose. Assess your life as it is. Look for things that you've always been good at doing, and the things that bring you joy and happiness. It could be cooking, writing, acting, fixing things, drawing, selling, whatever it is, it is your talent; **hone it!** You may be surprised by your discovery! Don't worry about how you will make money doing what you love; if you work with all your passion and do your very best, you will shine, and your gifts will make room for you.

Don't let anyone or anything hinder you from pursuing your dreams; that **includes yourself**. Many of us die with our dreams inside of us. Don't let your dreams go with you to your grave. Do what you love to do and explore ways to get paid for it!

Your journey has a purpose!

Landing in The Land of Plenty

By Jacob Fowler

You may notice my name on the front of the book. That's because I'm to co-editor co-creator along with my great friend Michael Bridgeman. It sure has been a challenging journey bringing this book to life. One that I have continued to be humbled and honored by. One that I've grown so much from, and I remain so excited for, as I know we are only just getting started. I hope you've been enjoying it so far, even more than that I hope it has brought you some value to you. I've said to myself throughout this project that if this book brings value to just one single person, then it will mission complete to me.... I secretly hope it can bring value to millions more.

In June of 1930 an advertisement in the 'Journal of the Professional Golfer's Association' appeared which stated 'Professional required for Barwon Heads Golf Club, Geelong, Victoria, Australia, Scotsman preferred, £150 per annum, house workshop rent free, passage paid to £40 Two years engagement, extending if suitable, if terminated within twelve months passage money to be repaid. Main qualification coach of outstanding ability, age limit 35. 'Dozens of applications were received from all over the world, and the 8th prime minister of Australia Stanley Bruce was enlisted to help select the right man for the job. The man selected was my great-great uncle (my grandmothers uncle) William Bud Russell, at the time he was 22 years young.

On the 5th of September Bud set sail on the Royal Mail S.S Mongolia, and what an adventure it must have been! Taking approximately 5 weeks stopping off in France, Egypt, Yemen, India, Sri Lanka, and various cities around Australia before arriving at its final destination and Bud's Melbourne. He arrived with 25 shillings in his pocket and some very big dreams, he wouldn't leave the shores of Australia again for many years and by then he would be a millionaire. He was and still is my inspiration.

Almost 85 years to the day later on October 15th, 2015, I departed from Birmingham to start a new life in Melbourne Australia, at this time I knew very little of Bud's legacy, but just like him I had some very big dreams and that same hungry entrepreneurial spirit! I checked in for my flight very early and using my charm had secured myself extra legroom seat for no extra cost being 6'4 this is always something to be glad about when you have a 22-hour flight ahead of you.

I had mixed feelings of excitement and sadness as I began to turn the pages of the notebook that had been passed around my leaving party a few days before, I felt overwhelmed as I began to read the pages. The warm tears began to stream down my face, the kind of tears that you really try to hold back because you're in a public place and you don't want to feel embarrassed. I soon found peace with letting them flow as I read all the kind, endearing and loving messages wishing me well on my new journey and my new life in Australia. I knew in my heart I was doing the right thing; I had procrastinated about executing on it for five years, always waiting for the perfect moment or time to make the move. There is no perfect moment or time. There will always be some form of resistance to any big change or decision you have to make. You have to seize opportunities when they present themselves, because time is the most precious thing we have, and no one has any time to waste.

"The credit belongs to the man who is actually in the arena, whose face is marred by dust and sweat and blood, who strives valiantly, who errs and comes up short again and again, because there is no effort without error or shortcoming, but who knows the great enthusiasms, the great devotions, who spends himself in a worthy cause; who, at the best, knows, in the end, the triumph of high achievement, and who, at the worst, if he fails, at least he fails while daring greatly, so that his place shall never be with those cold and timid souls who knew neither victory nor defeat."
- Theodore Roosevelt.

I was lucky enough to have explored lots of the world in my teens and early 20's, I always knew there was more to life then the town I grew up in (The Royal town of Sutton Coldfield) and as much as I loved my life there, I felt there was more for me in foreign lands. I had started to feel stagnant, and I was hungry for a new challenge. I knew that a plethora of new opportunities awaited me in Australia (the land of plenty) however that didn't stop self-doubt creeping in. I wondered as I flew across the world that night, how well I would manage being so far from my hometown, my family, and friends that I loved so dearly, from everything I knew to be comfortable, familiar, and safe. I wasn't sure I had made the right decision but what I did know was that everything I desired and wanted was on the other side of fear, and that by stepping out of my comfort zone in such a huge way would ultimately lead to massive growth.

"He still had doubts about the decision he had made. But he was able to understand one thing: making a decision was only the beginning of things. When someone makes a decision, he is really diving into a strong current that will carry him to places he had never dreamed of when he first made the decision." – Paula Coelho – The Alchemist.

In order to keep me focused and aligned on creating my dream life, I found myself getting into personal development and in touch with my spiritual side. I remember a friend of mine Dr Yury Shamis telling me *"Once you start on the journey of personal development it's a road that never ends."* It sounded bewildering and fascinating to me, and I dived right into it. I quickly became enthralled in the power of positive thinking, the law of attraction and manifestation, digesting as much material as I could on the subject and surrounding myself with people who did the same. This led me to realize that the creation of my future was in my own hands and with the right mindset and execution absolutely anything was possible. Ultimately what I desired was to achieve complete time and financial freedom, giving me the ability to live freely between Australia and the UK. I needed to create the perfect blend of lifestyle and environment without having to sacrifice regularly seeing my loved ones, instead I would bring them with me around the world and create wonderful memories together. I started writing a list of goals that I would need to achieve to make my dream a reality. This large and varied list had everything from small palatable goals to huge goals that scared the hell out of me. If your biggest goals don't scare you then you need bigger ones. There is little growth in achieving goals that don't require you to step outside your comfort zone. That's then when things start to get really fun, that's where the growth happens.

I quickly learnt to achieve my dream lifestyle I had to create multiple income streams, that operated globally, so that no matter where in the world I was, the money would keep coming in. Then I could stop trading my time for someone else's money and I would have attained what I truly desired, true financial and time freedom, living life on my own terms. *"If you don't learn how to make money in your sleep you'll work until you die"* - Warren Buffet. I keep multiple copies in my wallet, car and later stuck on my walls around my home. Subtle reminders of your goals are key. It's important to keep them in clear view everyday so they are present in your mind to motivate you in what you are working towards. When the tough times come and let me tell you they are going to, you need to be consistently reminded of your WHY!

My uncle Bud passed away in 1997 and I've been blessed to connect with some people that knew him, and I am continuing my research into his very colourful and inspiring life. He was a true spirited entrepreneur who hand made his own brand of 'Bud Russell' golf clubs as well as importing exclusive golf clothing and shoes from Scotland and London to be sold in Australia. Everything he did was planned and he was years ahead of his peers and his time. In 1977, Bud Russell was conferred Honorary Life Member of Barwon Heads Golf Club and was acknowledged among the Queen's Honours with a B.E.M. in 1982 for services to golf and his community. He also served in the RAAF in WWII reaching the rank of sergeant and was decorated for his military work.

I'm immensely proud to be related to this man and his legacy and I see myself in everything he did, it's my honour to follow in his footsteps and create a massive success of myself too. I had no idea how I was going to transition from my current career path as a humble plumber to that of an entrepreneur and global business owner. One thing I was sure of is that it would involve a lot of hard work, persistence, and patience. I had to stick with my current career path as a plumber working for a company for at least three years so that I could get my permanent residency, only then would I be free to own and operate my own business.

I've never been one to follow the rules and my insatiable appetite for the hustle didn't stop me creating various income streams alongside my day job. The only way to move forward in life is to think forward and keep trending in that direction. Only ever look backwards to see how far you've come and what you have achieved.

One day I was feeling frustrated and fed up with being fired from a job after a disagreement. It was still early days and it had taken me a while to secure the job, so I felt like I had taken one step forwards and two steps back. As I got home that evening and was completing some paperwork, I stumbled across a similarity that I took as a sign and one that gave me a lot of comfort. The Australia coat of arms depicts a Kangaroo and an Emu two animals that can only move forwards, thus symbolizing a nation that only moved forwards. The coat of arms for my home city of Birmingham, England is quite a different looking affair with a female artist and a man with a hammer and anvil; if you look carefully at the bottom of the insignia you can see the word FORWARD. In my moment of strife, I took this a sign from the universe and told myself 'Just keep moving forward Jake, you've got this.'

"Life is a fight for territory when you stop fighting for what you do want, what you don't want automatically takes over.' – Les Brown

Fast forward almost 6.5 years later to May 2022 and I've achieved many of my goals including the major one of freedom, to live between Australia and the UK. I've built my own highly successful global brand 'Paddock Blade', as well as being involved in a multitude of other businesses and projects. I've built a great network of cherished friends both here in Australia and across the world. I've seized opportunities to travel Australia and explore other parts of the world and even got involved in some not-for-profit projects such as Mission Rainwater a charity created by myself and others, which donated and installed over 80 rainwater tanks to families affected by the devastating 'Black Friday' Australian bush fires of 2019/2020.

The quiet time of 2020 allowed me to seize an opportunity that I had on my list of goals for a long-time. To be trained in public speaking by the world's greatest public speaker, Mr. Les Brown after joining a program Mr. Brown formed with Jon Talarico called the 'Power Voice'. It was a wonderfully fulfilling experience as well as an endearing journey that I thoroughly enjoyed. I learnt so much and vastly expanded my network globally. I worked hard and was chosen to be the first to speak at the inaugural Power Voice summit, which is how I came to meet so many of the wonderful people that are featured in this book. The title of my speech was 'The Hunger for the Hustle' which quickly became a podcast and now here we are today with this fantastic book which in turn ticks another life goal off the list for me to produce my own book!

Life is a journey full of wonderful surprises and with an open heart and mind you just never know where it's going to take you. With a clear intention, a great set of goals that scare and inspire you, paired with a lot of hard work patience and persistence. Absolutely anything you put your mind to is not only possible but probable. You can create the life of your dreams, whatever they may be for you, however they may look. It is your right to achieve them; no one else can achieve them for you but YOU! One vital thing I've learnt on my journey is the importance of having people around you that believe in you, back you all the way through the tough times as well as the tremendous. I'm not here to tell you it's going to be easy, as I have highlighted in this chapter it will at times be incredibly difficult, so having people around you who help you on the way and don't get in the way, is the key to success. In turn do the same for them and all ride the journey of greatness together. As you start ticking those goals off your list, if your anything like me or my great Uncle Bud in no time you'll be chasing a new goal for yourself. Keep moving forwards with that great momentum and remember, as much as you celebrate things big and small enjoy the journey as much as the destination.

"You can't climb the ladder of success with your hands in your pockets." – Arnold Schwarzenegger

At the young keen and able age of 34 years young my story is still being written. As my journey unfolds, I will have much more to share with you, as well as telling you more about my Uncle Bud's journey. But you'll have to wait for the next chapter of Hunger for the Hustle – Stories of Struggles to Success, to hear more about that! For now, I wish you massive success and continued greatness as you strive to achieve your goals, your dreams and whatever you want out of life. Most importantly above all else believe in yourself, stay healthy, stay happy, stay hungry and keep on hustling!

Before I go, I would like to give special thanks and mention to Michael Bridgeman who conceived the idea for this book. Without your time skills and energy, it would have never been possible. Also, to Irene Lihaven without your tireless work, patience, and persistence this book would not have been possible either. To the great skills and assistance of Denise Nicholson who got so many of our authors across the line. To Emiliana who got my own chapter across the line.

I would also like to thank my parents for their guidance and love, for backing me unconditionally and letting me choose my own path. As well as all my family and friends for the endless love, faith, and support on all my projects, however crazy they might be! My BIGGEST thanks goes to YOU for being kind and curious enough to purchase this book and in turn your support for the 'Beanies Arc'[15] charity (read more about the charity at the end of this book) that is truly close to my heart. I hope you got some value from this book. Be proud of yourself for making the investment in the greatest thing you can be in life.... YOURSELF.

"We invest our time, effort and energy in many things, people and places, but the biggest return you'll ever make will be from the investment you make in yourself."
– Jacob Fowler

Connect with me and follow my entrepreneurial journey @Jakehero7[16] | all platforms

Follow and subscribe to my podcast @hungerforthehustle[17] | all platforms

If you want to talk business then find me on LinkedIn | linkedin.com/in/JJFowler or email me at hello@hungerforthehustle.com I'm always excited and open to discuss new ventures and collaborations.

---

15. https://www.alicesarc.org/arc/beanie-evans

16. https://www.instagram.com/jakehero7

17. https://linktr.ee/Hungerforthehustle

Chase your Dreams

By Tarnya Cowley

If you had a chance to live life over again, would you do things differently?

Have you had a moment in your life where you thought, is this it? There must be more to life than this. And you had to decide whether to stay in your comfort zone or step out to grow and transform. The decision you make will determine whether you advance in life or retreat.

As a girl, I was scorned and rejected by people I respected, and thought should love me. I loved hanging out at the youth and community hall, where I regularly visited with my friends. This was my place of refuge and safety. I looked up to my leaders in the youth centre. Until the day that things took a turn.

I stood in the youth community hall, laughing and joking with my friends. We were pulling faces and making each other fall about with laughter, when out of the blue, I was met with, "Look at you! Look at you with those big goggle eyes! Carry on like that, and you'll see, you'll amount to nothing!" Those words hit me and shook me up. I froze for a moment because I couldn't believe who said it, it was one of the youth workers. I was just being me, having a laugh, hanging out with my friends, and having fun.

I never expected those words to leave his mouth. I had always thought my eyes were expressive before this insult. This particular worker began calling me into the office regularly for lectures on my attitude. I started to feel so self-conscious, and my self-esteem took a dive. Those were some damaging, hurtful words I was told. How can an adult speak to a child in that way? I held onto those words and believed the lies. I played them over in my mind. It became a self-fulfilling prophecy. If you hear something for long enough, you start to believe it. I pressed the repeat button as I was unsure how to press stop. Those words haunted me for years. They sliced like a knife. I doubted myself, and my self-esteem was severely affected. I lost my confidence. My dreams seemed like a distant memory.

I was lost in negative thoughts; if I tried to say something, I would be afraid that I would fail. The feeling of not being good enough was always there. Putting myself down was something I often did, sitting at the back of the class so I wouldn't be seen. Other people's opinion of me consumed me. I did not believe in *me;* I chose to listen to the negative voices. I would play them over and over in my head. Again, and again, the recorder in my mind was on repeat, unsure how to press stop. For years I didn't know who I was, assuming the identity that others gave me. I was walking around as an impostor.

We have the power to change our mindsets, the power to stay the same or move forward.

To escape the negativity, I would read books. *"It all begins and ends in your mind. What you give power to has power over you. If you allow it."*

Most people don't think they can change their mindset to think differently and achieve their goals and dreams. If you chase anything in life, chase the things that get you excited about living!

When I looked at where I was, I had to transform my mindset to change and transform. I had goals I wanted to achieve. But there was no way that I could reach them. Well, so I thought. My mindset was destructive, and I needed to rebuild it with positive thoughts. If I wanted to make changes, I had to count on myself and be the change I wanted to see.

I heard a voice, *'rise above your circumstances and situations, pursue your goals and dreams.'*

I had a choice to make: Continue to let life pass me by and pale into insignificance or be strong, be courageous and achieve whatever I put my mind to.

When I heard that voice in my head, it was a jarring experience for me. I had to challenge myself to work on my mindset daily. That voice was like a constant reminder that I needed to decide.

When I look back over my life, there are things I denied myself because I wasn't willing to fight. One of my favourite sayings, '...*be transformed by the renewing of your mind.*' from Romans 12:2. I affirmed myself with positive affirmations,

'I can do ALL things through Christ, who gives me strength.'

'I am more than a conqueror'.

I drew strength from the words in the Bible. It comforted me and gave me peace of mind. In that moment, I decided, "enough is enough. Now is the time to take action!" It all started with having self-belief. I held onto the words my mum used to say to me,

"Tarnya, you are fearfully and wonderfully made."

I made a conscious choice and spoke out those positive affirmations each day. This allowed me to see the true power in my voice; this was when I knew I wanted to use my voice to empower. I was encouraged to look at myself in the mirror and make those declarations. That was very difficult to do because I didn't want to look at myself. But I knew that this was not optional. This was a case of an emergency! In doing this, my confidence soared.

I set goals for myself, and I took opportunities with both hands. I took the chance to move to a different city with one suitcase and a one-way coach ticket. I enrolled into a degree programme to become a qualified teacher. I made a committed decision that I will complete this programme no matter how hard it gets. Perseverance paid off, and I had a career as a successful lecturer for 15 years.

I felt the urgency to move on. I felt there was more for me to do. On January 1st, 2018, I took pen to paper and wrote my book *Open Doors*. Six weeks later, the book was complete. A few months later, I became a bestseller on Amazon. I handed in my notice at work and embarked on a new journey, becoming a coach and a motivational speaker. It ignited the passion in me. And that same fire in me, I wanted to use to help others chase those dreams and dream again.

You can achieve your goals. You do not have to believe what other people have said about you. I needed to get out of my own way to realise what was possible. I am now living my purpose. It came naturally to me to support others and help individuals get unstuck and chase their dreams. I became overwhelmed with people requesting me to help them achieve their lifelong goals. Steve Harvey quoted: "*Your career is what you're paid for. Your calling is what you're made for.*" I found pleasure in helping women fine-tune their vision and be unstoppable as they pursued their goals. Helping them get unstuck, set goals, and take action.

Today is the day that you serve notice to the circumstances that have held you back. Dream again; what is it you *really* want? Write your desires and act on them.

You *can* do more than you could ever think or imagine! And you've got to demand more out of yourself. There comes a point in our lives when we know a change has got to take place.

We have the power to change. I decided that the Tarnya I had been, no longer served me. I served notice to a negative outlook. I served notice to rejection and low self-esteem. There comes the point in our lives that we must choose. We must choose to stop believing the lies and dare to dream again. Do not let the past define who you are or who you thought you were. You are free to be you; you are fearfully and wonderfully made!

Chase those dreams, achieve your goals.

Now I've decided to "*accept what is, let go of what was, and have faith in what will be.*" (Sonia Ricotti.) I am a Les Brown certified speaker, embracing my newfound confidence. I am regarded as a respected and influential speaker. I have over 17 years' experience speaking on different platforms. I have a down to earth approach to empower and help individuals live a life of purpose. I am also a Personal Development Coach. I have authored three books, and I am the author of the bestselling book, *Open Doors*. I have just released my newest publication, *Plan it. See it. Anticipate it.*

'*A year from now, you will wish you had started today.*' Karen Lamb.

Plan it. See it. Anticipate it.

Do you have something that you want to achieve in your life? Today is the day to make that bold step and chase your dreams!

Get in touch today.

ibelieveican.co.uk/contact/[18]

---

18. https://ibelieveican.co.uk/contact/

The Sneaky Lie That Holds Entrepreneurs Back

And, could be standing in your way right now!

By Michael Bridgman

I couldn't believe what I was hearing.

I was standing at the front of a room, full of hungry and eager entrepreneur clients, many of whom we're just getting their businesses rolling…and I couldn't believe what I'd heard.

It was total bullshit!

But, before I get to why I was so shocked, let me introduce myself. My name is Michael Bridgman, editor of Hunger for the Hustle Volume 1 and a serial entrepreneur. I'd like to personally thank you for taking the time to read this compilation work and I hope you're loving every page of it.

I spent hours, days in fact, thinking and journaling about what best to share with you in my chapter of this book.

My options swung from doling out hard-knock business advice, to sharing the power of finding your WHY, over to giving away my five key marketing fundamentals. I even wrote an entire article on how to be more productive.

But that's not where I decided to go with this…

I decided I'd help you overcome one of the most dangerous lies nearly every entrepreneur must overcome to be successful.

A lie that holds many of us back from achieving great things.

A lie that saps our energy and dissolves our focus.

A lie that takes root in our psyche early and festers and rots there.

And this is a lie that has helped seed and grow a trendy belief in and around entrepreneurship, that creates false and ridiculous expectations, that puts many of us behind in our ventures even before we start.

Being at the front of that room was an honour I was given after completing an intense two-year business education program and building a successful brick-and-mortar business with my family.

At that point, the family business was really thriving, and it afforded me the free time to take my experience and education and help others.

Now, you might be wondering what is this lie?

It's a lie that pretty much all of us have heard.

It's been told to us, over and over again, by our parents, our families, our teachers, coaches, and many others.

In fact, it was because of my belief in this false promise that I walked away from my first, promising career and I was left penniless and confused.

This lie is...

"Do what you love, and you'll never work a day in your life."

This is a complete myth.

Success takes WORK!

The person in my class who'd stood up and shared their challenge said something that you've probably heard before, perhaps even said before. I know I'd said it, before I understood what I'm about to share with you.

They said that they were losing their passion for what they were doing. That the days were starting to feel like *work* and that they didn't understand why. They said that they were told going into business for themselves was going to be easy and they could just do what they loved to do, and it would never feel like hard work.

This wonderful young businessperson was very talented, and their work was fantastic. But they were starting to slip down a slope of self-doubt, fueled by this ridiculous misconception that doing what you love should never feel like work.

I had been watching this person stop and start in their business for a while. There were times when they'd be making great strides and progress. Their business revenues would be rising, their marketing would be working, and their sales would be flowing, and everything would be looking great. But then only a few weeks later they'd be sliding into a rut again, struggling with their motivation, losing deals, and missing deadlines.

I remember thinking to myself in one of our roundtables with this person, why can't they just find some consistency?

At that moment when they shared this frustration with the group, I looked around the room and it's what I saw that shocked me so much; many others were nodding in agreement with them.

Could all these entrepreneurs really believe that building a business was going to be sunshine and roses every single day, just because they were following their passion?

Could they really believe that doing something they cared about as a business was going to open a door to a whole new world, where they never again felt like they were doing hard work?

The simple answer is...yes, that's what they thought.

This is the common trap so many of us fall into when we decide to go into business for ourselves. We believe in the lie that doing something we enjoy doing ensures that it never feels like work and that's just not true at all.

You ask any successful person, no matter the field; athlete, artist, entrepreneur etc... you ask them if they loved every moment of every practice, rehearsal, late night, early morning and they'll all tell you *'Heck no'!*

In fact, we'd think they were nuts if they did.

But they'll also all tell you that the WORK was worth it.

So, if these people, who reach the peak of their fields, don't love the work every day, why should we expect that of ourselves.

And this is where the problems start, unfair expectations

The young business owner in my class was working with a false equation and it wasn't their fault.

The equation they believed in was:

Doing What You Love = Never Feeling Like Your Working

This statement is completely B.S., but for many of us, it's hard-wired into our brains.

So, when their business venture started to get hard, when they ran into difficult challenges and the everyday commitment started to feel more like a grind than a fun-filled merry-go-round, this false equation would show up like the little devil on their shoulder and say...

"Well, this is starting to feel like work, it's not supposed to feel like work, so maybe you're not actually passionate about this...which means maybe you should have never gone into business in the first place and you're probably not very good at this and you should've just stayed at your job like your arrogant Uncle Rob told you to..."

From here the spiral into frustration and confusion is inevitable and I know this because I suffered from it many times in my own life. In fact, I gave up a promising career as an actor because the hours and hours of rehearsal, the auditions and all the time you need to spend practicing and learning your craft, all began to feel like *work* to me...and I thought it wasn't supposed to, so I walked away from my career.

This false pre-tense left me broke, confused and battling depression. I remember thinking to myself; If this acting thing feels like work, then clearly, I don't really love it and if I don't love acting...then I have no idea who I am or what to do!

I found myself stuck between two battling beliefs. The belief that doing something I was passionate about shouldn't feel like work and the belief that success only comes to those who work hard.

I was caught in this tug of war between these two viewpoints, and this is where I see so many entrepreneurs also find themselves snared and leads to the roller coaster ride they feel like they're on.

Maybe you find yourself caught in the same trap, stuck on that same roller coaster.

There is a way out.

After nearly five years of coaching business owners and after battling through this false pretense myself I can promise you there are keys to unlocking yourself from the shackles of this lie. Unfortunately, the number of different keys that you could use to unlock yourself could fill an entire book and I only have one short chapter to share with you, so I'm going to focus on the one that changed things the most for me in my career in business.

Change the Equation!

One of the key concepts I coach my clients on is 'become Passionate About the Client, Not the Work'.

Fundamentally business is simpler than we make it.

A business delivers a transformation to a client...that's it.

Whether it's making them a sandwich and a coffee, selling them a car, curing an illness, solving pain, or delivering an experience...each and every business gives a transformation to a client.

And, from all my experience in business and helping business owners, the quickest way to get them out of the 'If I love it, it can't be work, but it needs to 'be work' to be successful' mindset trap is to get them to shift their perspective from 'I love the work' to 'I love transforming my clients'.

When you make this viewpoint change everything becomes clearer.

Now, that 'hard work' it takes to become successful makes sense, because that hard work is focused on helping someone else and delivering on what you've promised. You are no longer the focus of the 'hard work', your client is.

So what's the new equation?

Doing What You Love = Transforming Peoples Lives

Standing at the front of that room, with over 30 entrepreneurs at tables in front of me, I asked that business owner if she loved the difference she made in her client's lives?

She replied "*Yes, of course*".

Then I said, "*That's what you should be passionate about*".

As an entrepreneur, there will be days where you're infatuated and in love with every moment of what you're doing and then there will be days where you despise each second of it.

I have found that if you are truly hungry for success, if you truly want to have an impact and you want to do that through business (which I'm guessing you do because you're reading this book) then one of the first challenges you must overcome is to burn away this notion that '*doing what you love, will never feel like work*'.

Because, my friend, as soon as you turn what you love into a business, there will be days where you won't love it and it's going to feel like work, hard, very hard work.

And what will see you through those hard days will be your passion and love for the client and how you've transformed their lives, not for the work itself.

Put another way...fall more in love with the Why and Who of what you do and less with the How, the What and the Where and you'll find that consistency and resiliency you need to make what you love into a successful business.

Thanks so much for reading.

Michael Bridgman

CEO TYME Marketing & Consulting

michaelbridgman.ca[19]

---

19. https://d.docs.live.net/4927f85f42ada7cc/Documents/www.michaelbridgman.ca

Knock Out That Unexpected Opponent

By Eric Collier

One thing that I have learned in life is: there will come a time when we find ourselves under pressure with our backs against a wall, facing an unexpected opponent. When the pressure is on, what do you do? I believe we develop this "Go-To Solution" that becomes a problem-solving method we rely on. Whether right or wrong, success or failure, when the pressure hits, we either succumb or instinctively resort to operating in that solution.

There is a quote that says, "*adversity introduces a person to who he is.*" Therefore, when things are at their worst, a person's actions or reactions will reveal what he/she is made of. Some questions that used to float around in my head when I faced a quandary were: Are you a man, or are you a mouse? Are you going to stand up and take responsibility, to face your problems head-on? Or are you going to scurry into a hole to hide, and wait in fear?

What is your "Go-To solution" when things get tough? I used to waver between, scurrying into a hole, or stand Brave and face the foe. **No longer!**

I can thank Tuesday, November 26, 2013, for that change because it started a 352-day life lesson I will never forget. It was the day I lost my job and the six-figure salary I had worked so hard for.

It was two days before we were to celebrate "Thanksgiving," and it was time to turn in my badge and be walked out the door. I knew the day was coming because my company had just lost the contract, but I was not worried, **I had a plan!**

Initially, I believed I would walk away with my severance, and vacation pay; then return with the same job title, as an employee of the new company.

Well as we all know, **<u>OUR PLAN IS NOT ALWAYS THE PLAN</u>**. Attempt after attempt passed and I was never rehired. Little did I know that it was the beginning of what would be a 352-day emotional rollercoaster ride of unexpected battles.

I couldn't figure out what went wrong. I remembered thinking, *what happened, they always rehire*? I had it all planned out because they needed my expertise. Instead of giving up completely, I kept hoping that they'd come to their senses. It took me some time, but I finally got the message that I needed to start applying to other companies for jobs in my field.

Nothing happened the first few weeks, but I wasn't worried. I had some savings, a part-time job, and I knew, with my skills, a job opportunity would come soon. Little did I know that my job search would eventually turn into a 352-day marathon. When I did not get a job by the time I expected, an **unfamiliar opponent** reared its ugly head and started to harass me.

He started telling me the reason I didn't get the job was because I wasn't good enough; and I didn't belong in those high-paying jobs in the first place.

I admit, for a while, I began to believe him.

After watching my big-time plan fall apart, I woke up to the reality that the fight I was in was real, and it was bigger than just me getting a job. As the holiday season ended and the new year began, big tolls were piling up, and money was running low. I was working seven days a week doing more than full-time hours on my part-time job, and still not making ends meet.

Meanwhile, in my head, my opponent's voice began to get louder and meaner. As things got worse, other unexpected opponents showed up. I knew I had to strategize to win this battle.

Losing was not an option!

To add insult to injury, my wife fell into her own battle with depression and anxiety, and she can tell her own story, but our two journeys combined created emotional and physical dark rocky days for both of us. I did not understand what my wife was going through, and in hindsight, I could have handled situations much better. At times I questioned if our marriage would survive.

Additional pressure was added when the opponent I was facing called in reinforcements: adding **bad credit** in place of my six-figure salary. Causing job offers to come and go. I would be hired and fired before I could even start. I'd be excited the pain was about to end one minute and go back to "damn another SETBACK" the next.

Having had financial issues before, it was never so bad that it interfered with my job. In my head, this opponent was kicking my butt, "Ready to give up? "What now?" "Are you a man or are you a mouse?" It was frustrating.

I couldn't get that crap out of my head.

No matter how much I tried to explain my circumstances to recruiters, it would fall on deaf ears, and I had to start the process all over again. It was driving me nuts, and there were days when I just wanted to shake somebody and say, "**Can't you see what's going on?**"

Although I kept telling my wife that we would get through it; when I was by myself, the pressure, stress, and the weight of it all, sometimes became emotionally overwhelming; and at times I would break down. I struggled with stopping those vitriol thoughts, but I knew for sure that where they were leading me, I was not trying to go.

I had to keep my sanity. I had to fight through it!

I had to dig down deep inside to find the strength, and courage to fight against the negative thoughts that were bombarding me. **Rejecting and repudiating them became my focus.** I also realized that I needed to reshape my thinking and not focus on what was going wrong. I consciously made the decision not to focus on the bills that were coming in daily; neither was I going to hide from the bill collectors who kept calling. I boldly spoke to them; my last conversation with a bill collector who asked when they would get their money, went, "I don't know. When I get a job and have the money, you'll get it." I told my wife, "From here on out, I'm only focusing on what I can control, to hell with everything else."

I began listening to a recording of "The Power of Positive Thinking", by the renowned Norman Vincent Peale. I didn't know what to expect but I began to practice some of the things Dr. Peale recommended: I began to see problems as opportunities and thanked God for them. I thanked him for things I saw in our future as if I had already received them. **I talked positively, prayed fervently, and expected greatly.**

Things changed, and my wife noticed the difference in me; and honestly, I noticed it too. She also began to speak positively about all the things she struggled with, and the things we faced; whether she understood them or not, and before long, she too was at peace with herself. Her laughter permeated the house once again, and I enjoyed every sound of it. When it was all said and done, we were still standing, but THE OPPONENT WAS DEFEATED!

At a time when I thought I was just creating a coping mechanism to get through a very tough time, I gained a new mindset: I started thinking positively and speaking things into being.

I learned that the mind is incredible, and we become what we think about. **What a blow to the opponent!**

When I thought I was not good enough, I was not, and I couldn't get the jobs I wanted. When I affirmed that I was good enough, I was good enough.

Life's battle is in the mind; you either control it or it controls you. It took 352 days of experience, growth, and learning, but it was all worth it. I now have a great career and I help at-risk teens prepare for a successful future.

It takes a lot of courage to push through hard times. Sometimes we just need to **Adjust Mindset & Perspective: AMP It Up** to get back on track. My challenge to you is: take a timeout to assess your thoughts and daily operations. What is your "Go-To" solution when problems arise? What areas of life do you focus on, positive or negative? Are outside influences dictating your moods and actions? Are you making decisions to get things back to normal or move to the next level? Are you a man, woman, or a mouse?

I am living proof that when you change your mindset, you change your outcome. As the Good Book says, *"For as he thinketh in his heart, so is he."* I encourage you to give it a try: when life pushes you up against a wall, be strong! AMP It Up and JUST KEEP PUSHING!

C. Eric Collier is a Motivational Speaker, Life Coach, Philanthropist, and Author. His mission: inspire others to shed the "old you" to meet the "new you." Mental toughness is key. His driving mantra, **"I Just Keep Pushing, because nobody will do it for me."** *Schedule a free 30min coaching session, speaker requests, or receive advanced event notices at 1momentumshift.com/book-c-eric-collier*[20]

---

20. https://www.1momentumshift.com/book-c-eric-collier

Keeping It On the Rails

5 Vital Keys to Riding the Roller Coaster of Entrepreneurship

By Keith Lloyd

Thirty-five years of entrepreneurship. Roller coaster rides, rebirths, and learning. LOTS of learning. And never a dull moment. I wouldn't change any of it. In reading this chapter you will learn some of my most vital moments that shifted me and as a result, give you, the reader, the knowledge required to do whatever it takes to achieve your own success. And you'll have the assurance that no matter what, you can get through any challenge you decide to take on. Please read on...

In 1986, I started my first business. By accident really. I was waiting for a carpentry apprenticeship and literally fell into a business launch due to a desperate need for rent money. I started from nothing – complete scratch. A friend co-signed for a loan for me from the bank to get started and there I was, completely mesmerised, and with no business education. My background was in the food industry and so I partnered up with a former co-worker and started a food manufacturing business – packaged sushi to be exact. We started with a unique recipe, some good financial information and drive. Yes, as the title of the book alludes to, I was HUNGRY!

We started out by selling to small fish stores on Vancouver's West Side and over the years built our enterprise into a highly successful business supplying every single grocery chain, film set, hospital, and we even snagged an airline! At our peak, we were creating over 10,000 pieces of sushi a day and shipping out this highly perishable product throughout the province of British Columbia, Canada. All of this done from an industrial kitchen of approximately 600 square feet. And I had started with basically nothing. Crazy beginnings but anyone can do it – even you!

Through our 20 years of business, my company was forced to learn how to create great systems, processes, and structure. Operations manuals, flow charts, logistics...everything. Growth will do that to you when your business demands it so be prepared and open to grow. And nothing was a slam dunk in the first iteration. In all of this, it required a lot of perseverance, resilience, and passion. I loved what had been created! Have you ever felt so passionate about something that you knew for certain it was where you were supposed to be? I felt like this for a long time. And then things started to unravel.

Remember the rollercoaster ride? By 2006, I was burnt out, partnerless, and at a crossroads – have you ever had one of THOSE moments? Have you ever been in an ugly situation in your business or worse, in your life?

This was mine.

I had a young family and my time, freedom, and money – all the things that success had brought – were waning. Profits shrinking (**Valuable lesson here: Profits are all that matter – your top line just feeds your ego**), no time for my 2 daughters and wife, and tied by the chains of my business (so it felt at that time). So, I sold the business. Got out. Lost my identity of 20 years and sat there on day 1 post-business and wondered what I was going to do: not a clue.

AND YET....

That entrepreneurial spirit was still there. This is where your passion, intestinal fortitude, resilience, and action will drive you crazy, because you know you're destined for better than where you are in that moment. And here I was in my unsure moment...but I jumped anyway.

When my world was crumbling, I made a big decision: I would rebuild in a vastly different realm and would be successful there too. And it was going to take a lot. Time, energy, patience, and compassion for myself. This is when my journey as an entrepreneur truly started.

The first thing I looked at was: what do I have: skillsets, experience, expertise? Then: What was it that I LOVED about my first business? What sucked? And above all, where could I take all this information moving forward? Having a young family factored in as well. Providing for my household was critical for me. My wife of that time was not able to provide for our home long term (if you do have this factor, you have a decided advantage).

What I learned about selling my business: It affects more than just the business owner and their family. It affects suppliers cashflow, customer's revenues (retail clients), and above all: the families of my employees. This was devastating for me. And what I realised was that I knew that it was not the first time this had happened to an entrepreneur. It happens all the time! And sadly, it demoralises people. Dreams get crushed, recovery is often slow, and retirements become a pipe dream. I hated this. Especially when I knew that I had the knowledge to prevent this more often than not. So, I decided to go into consulting.

Turns out it was an easy decision based on my experiences, but I knew nothing about how to go about this. I had been selling a product, not a service in my first business. I went and took a consulting program. Beyond that, I had tools but no business structure. I realised that this wasn't uncommon for start-ups. So, I developed a system that evolved and kept evolving. It included dialogues with entrepreneurs and people wanting to start a business.

Another thing I learned at this time: grow your network! Find GOOD people that have expertise and experience doing the things you don't know. And ask for their opinion and their help. Most good people are willing to help a little. And when you need a lot of their help: pay them – or trade services...or work for them – even Think and Grow Riches author Napoleon Hill did this. Do this and you will accelerate your path to success.

So, I did just this. I joined a good networking group who helped me a ton. And I got work with one of them while I grew my consulting business. Big steps forward. And with all of this, I got to support those businesses by using their services. And over the years I have discovered and refined what makes my consulting business unique and incorporated that into my message when chatting with people.

Learning didn't just happen at the professional level. I took a series of personal development programs. Years later, I realised: the more I learned about myself and worked out the crap, the healthier a mind I had, which translated to better business decisions. And 12 years later I still have a number of those friendships that started in those programs – some of them have even become clients!

And I am always growing and looking to expand my learning and my network. Now in 2021, I am feeling like I am back at the top of my game and in a zone. My vision of rebuilding my success in a different realm has materialized.

Here are 5 key elements that if you want to take your success to a brand-new level, that I discovered while taking this "Part 2" journey to my success:

1. You are either a Visionary or a Doer. It is HIGHLY DIFFICULT to be both.
2. When the time is right, hire people that **don't** do the same thing you do (i.e., Duplicate yourself). Hire those that compliment your vision and let them do what they are great at. No phenomenally successful entrepreneur has ever become that doing everything by himself, so build your team and support them as much as they support you and your dream.
3. Never be afraid to ask for support and be enthusiastic about helping others. This grows your reputation for not knowing it all and willing to see others become successful.
4. Build a foundation for your business to grow on – do the work to create your message, build a scalable business. And be financially responsible while taking calculated risks. And "just jump" even when you are uncomfortably fearful. "You miss all of the shots you never take" ~ Michael Jordan
5. Your business is not your life. It is a small but important part of it. Remember those people and the away from work activities that mean the most to you. THIS is what you should work towards immediately. Not: "when success comes". Life is too short, and God help you if you leave this Earth without enjoying it while you are here.

Today, 14 years after I started my business consulting practice, I have so many good things in my life that I am profoundly grateful for. I have a new wife & 7-month-old son, many deep, meaningful friendships, and 7 members of my business team. We have helped countless businesses find success and balance – something that I am enormously proud of! And I am honored and thankful to be part of this book.

And now, with a span of the 35 years of entrepreneurship, I feel I can honestly say that I have found myself. I have come to a place in my life of contentment. I have found peace and happiness FINALLY because I have found my calling and purpose. I urge you to find **your** purpose, find **your** passion, and monetize it! Life is too short to spend even a moment doing something you experience grief in. People need you! They need your knowledge and expertise. So, get out there and find your joy! And if you already have, spread it to others and GIVE BACK. THAT is part of your underlying purpose as a human being in this world.

And if you need guidance, structure, and help to fulfill your vision, feel free to contact me for a quick chat. Or visit our website BusinessSurgeon.ca[21] for some free resources to help you smooth out some of those potholes along your path – something that I am very familiar with...and good luck! You can do it!

Thanks for reading my story,

Keith

---

21. http://www.businesssurgeon.ca

From a GED to a PH.D.

By Dr. David A Spencer

I was supposed to wind up on the streets, in jail and in an early grave.

But I wound up inspiring others, earning a PHD and discovering a life full of purpose.

Did you know that every year, over 1.2 million students drop out of high school in the United States alone? That's one student every 26 seconds or 7,000 a day.

7000…every day.

In the US high school dropouts commit about 75% of crimes.

On any given day, about one in every 10 young high school dropouts are in jail or juvenile detention facilities. Over 80% of the incarcerated population is high school dropouts. Numbers are higher for dropouts of color.

I was a high school dropout.

In the year 1969 at the age of 16, I walked out of school unconcerned about my future. The theme of the decade was…*"It's your thing- do what you want to do!"*

So, I did!

There was a lot going on in the sixties…the Vietnam war, The Civil Rights Movement, The Hippie Movement, The Black Panther Party, The British Invasion, sex, drugs, rock & roll, Watergate, and Kent State!

It was a very confusing and unstable time!

I thought I could make it on my own, that I was pretty cool, and it was going to be easy, fun and exciting and it was for a while, then the excitement wore off and reality set in. It wasn't long before I was in survival mode.

I didn't think about or take into consideration what I would encounter after I dropped out of high school. Things I didn't think about like making a living, buying clothes, food, and a finding place to live. I was arrogant and I took it all for granted.

After 17 years of bad choices, I had had enough. I decided I was going to take my life, because I didn't see a way out of where I was stuck and felt like I had nothing to live for.

But, at the last minute I made a different choice. I decided to become a believer, a born-again Christian.

Until I received Christ I had issues, like low self-esteem and low self-confidence. To put it simply "I had a bad attitude."

As my self-confidence and self-esteem returned my desire to learn more about God led me to Bible school. But in order to be accepted I needed a High School diploma, which I didn't have. So I enrolled in the local adult GED program.

It's so important to find people who see you as more than how you see yourself. It's one of the reasons I believe God is so powerful, He sees more in us than we do.

But God comes to us through people, through the acts of others and He blessed me with some incredible people that helped me see more in me than I had before.

One of those people was a teacher I had, Mrs. Morris. When I needed to get my GED so I could get into Bible School she began to coach me. She began to mentor me. She believed in and encouraged me and when they announced the date for the test, I became anxious, but she said, *"You can do it Dave","* You're ready", *"I believe in you!"*

I didn't think I was ready, but I didn't want to let Mrs. Morris down so when she asked, I said "ok."

I passed that test and it sparked an unquenchable belief in myself and love of education and higher learning. I continued on to CFNI Bible Institute in Dallas, TX. where I received an Associates Degree.

While there I met another one of those people who saw more in me than I did, Dr. Walter Axtell.

Dr. Axtel began to coach and mentor me personally. He challenged and encouraged me to pursue my education to the highest level. He sent my transcripts to another seminary where I was accepted and received a Bachelor of Theology degree, Masters of Divinity degree and a Ph.D. in "The Philosophy of Pastoral Counseling."

At the graduation service the Dean of the seminary asked me if I would consider becoming an extended faculty member / teacher which I humbly accepted. It was an opportunity to give back, to inspire and encourage the students as they pursued their purpose, reached for their dreams, followed their hearts, set goals, and allowed themselves to imagine and believe they could accomplish anything they put their minds to as they focused on their destiny. It was a blessing being a part of their journey. That year I had the honor of helping over 125 students graduate with associate degrees, one of the proudest years of my life.

I felt a calling to pay my transformation forward and use my experience to help and inspire the lives of many, many others.

Their journeys inspire me. Journeys like Robert's, a man who served time in prison, homeless, on food stamps and buried in unhealthy relationships. A man who had no job and no prospects, who, after working and living with me embraced the love of Christ, got his life back and is now a living testament to incredible transformation.

Or journeys like Michael's, who at 15 years old was already on the wrong side of the law and whom I met in a juvenile detention centre, 35 years ago. With the work both him and I did together he righted the ship of his life, received Christ, married an amazing person, has an incredible family and runs his own business.

Because I decided to let go of my frailty and my fears, to pursue my purpose and treat my life like the gift it is, thousands of lives have been changed for the good.

We truly don't know the ripple effect we have when we live full and on purpose.

In fact, we even affected an entire town when we bought an old bar and converted it into a church. Our good work repelled the underhanded and criminal activity that had plagued the area. Business, new development, and an entirely re-vitalized community was developed.

I share with you these stories not to impress you but to encourage you to go for it, don't quit, change your paradigm and your perspective. There's greatness inside of you, you are special, fearfully, and wonderfully made with a skill set all your own, a voice that needs to be heard.

You will have to invest time and money in yourself. Get around people who have been where you want to go, ask questions, get involved with a community of people who think the same, who will challenge you, people you can be accountable to, and attend conferences. Invest in yourself!

It will initially cost you time, money, friends and even some family members but when they see you struggling, persevering, getting back up after each knock down, yet getting closer and closer to your destiny they will be challenged to look at their lives and (hopefully) begin to change, to pursue their purpose from your example.

Mr. Zig Ziglar said... *"Getting knocked down in life is a given. Getting up and moving forward is a choice."*

People will be watching! Some cheering you on, others hoping to see you fail but you will not fail because you're a winner! You will reach your destiny and then reach back and help others do the same.

My favorite book says this...

Jeremiah 29:11 *"For I know the plans and thoughts I have for you, says the Lord, plans for peace and well- being not for disaster, to give you a future and a hope."*

One of my coaches, Mr. Les Brown said, *"No matter how bad it is or how bad it gets I am going to make it."*

TEACHERS - THE STUDENTS NEED YOU

I'd like to encourage you with this famous poem by John Greenfield Whitter entitled...

"Don't Quit."

When things go wrong, as they sometimes will,

when the road you're trudging seems all uphill,

when the funds are low and the debts are high,

and you want to smile but you have to sigh,

when care is pressing you down a bit - rest if you must, but don't you quit.

Life is strange with its twists and turns

As every one of us sometimes learns

And many a failure comes about

When you might have won had you stuck it out.

Don't give up though the pace seems slow—You may succeed with another blow.

Success is failure turned inside out - the silver tint of the clouds of doubt,

and when you never can tell how close you are,

it may be near when it seems afar.

so, stick to the fight when you're hardest hit - it's when things seem worst, that you must not quit!

"You can begin again"

Education with revelation results in transformation – Dr David A. Spencer

Be encouraged, the best is yet to come!

Dr. David A Spencer

Kingdom Mindset Development

Let's Talk About It

A Christ Centered Counseling, Coaching & Discipleship Program

Drdavidspencer.com[22]

---

22. http://www.drdavidspencer.com

A Prescription for Joy & Happiness

By Fernanda Castaneda

I remember it like it was yesterday. A single phone call was about to shatter my world. Prior to February 2014, I remember being a happy young woman, living a good life with my two children and my husband (at that time). Everything seemed perfect and I felt I had it all. I was pursuing my dream of becoming a Nurse Practitioner and working as a nurse in a fast-paced urgent care center. I was on top of the world.

That world was forever changed on that cold day in February 2014 when I received the call. My father in Colombia said I have something I need to tell you. That news would rip my heart and bring me such emotional pain and suffering that for many days I felt like I wanted to die. I had never experienced anything like this before. The words he spoke to me brought me such an intense emotional pain that I couldn't breathe, and my life was thrown upside down.

My closest brother, Juan Miguel, with whom I had a special bond and relationship, had fallen sick and been rushed to the hospital. Nobody could figure out what was wrong with him, not the nurses, doctors, family, and friends could understand what was happening. After the test results came back, we came to learn that his heart was only working at nine percent of its capacity. He was 32 years old and was in great physical health all of his life. What was most shocking is nobody could give any answers as to what was causing this. Test after test and yet nothing.

I remember feeling so helpless, living in the United States, thousands of miles away and there wasn't anything I could do. The doctors kept Juan Miguel there in the hospital for several days and were finally able to get him stabilized enough to be discharged. His life was forever changed. He was under the care of a team of specialists and cardiologists and forced to take a number of heart medications. Even the simple task of getting up from a chair was now a challenge.

I felt a sense of relief knowing that he was now home and there seemed to be hope as he was now stable and was gradually improving. That relief was short-lived as he eventually was placed on a heart transplant list, continued to deteriorate, and eventually, a major part of me was gone on January 3rd, 2018.

When I thought things couldn't get any worse, I was blindsided by more damaging news that would take me to a deeper state of despair. On an early July morning, I discovered that the man I trusted with all of my being, had violated that trust and was having an affair. Everything I thought about our relationship was a complete illusion.

In a matter of months, I went from being a happy and loving person to being overcome by extreme emotions of anxiety and depression. I started having panic attacks, I couldn't sleep. I was unable to think clearly and couldn't even take care of myself or my children. I went from being a nurse who did not believe in depression or anxiety to being a person who was paralyzed with these feelings and emotions that were so debilitating I couldn't get out of bed for days at a time.

I did not know how to deal with these emotions and didn't have the tools I needed on how to help myself. I failed to understand how the power of the mind could actually help change my present reality. Instead, I spent the next 5 years in emotional pain and suffering. I was in counseling, taking four different prescriptions for depression and anxiety, and felt like I was in an endless black hole with no way out. I started to believe that this was how my life was now going to be like the new normal because I simply did not know what to do. I had fleeting moments of joy and happiness when I would dance, however that was just a temporary escape to what I saw as a permanent reality.

And then it happened.

I was driving to work one morning, beating myself up as usual about what a hypocrite I was. Here I was consulting with patients, diagnosing them, and giving them the treatment they needed to live a healthier and happier life, yet I was drowning in unhappiness and self-pity. I was desperate at this point and had hit rock bottom. There were moments when I wanted the pain to end and on that one day, in desperation, I started screaming out loud in my car. "Please, please, help me feel better. I can't feel like this anymore. What can I do to feel better? How else can I help myself?".

On the way home that day out of nowhere I saw a video on YouTube pop up on my phone. The video was, "The Strangest Secret" by Earl Nightingale. I had never heard of him, but something spoke to me that day and said listen. That video changed my life.

After I finished watching it, I understood immediately that only I was responsible for my well being, that I had created the reality that I was now living in, and only I could get myself out by going inward and working on myself, my thoughts, and on my mind.

I understood at that very moment that every thought that I was allowing in my mind had an equal emotion which was making me feel the way I was feeling all along. I had created this reality and only I could create a different one for myself. I immediately started immersing myself in everything I could find about personal growth.

I started listening to videos by Les Brown, Bob Proctor, Jim Rohn, Tony Robbins, Napoleon Hill, Dr. Joe Dispenza, Dr. Wayne Dyer, and others. I started reading books about personal development and the mind. I started going to seminars and within three months I was able to transform my life and be reborn all over again.

I stopped all of the medications I was taking, and I became very conscious of every thought I was allowing in my mind. I became so vigilant with my thoughts and emotions that when a negative thought would show up, I would start doing anything to get me in a better state of mind. The battle to regain my life was and continues to be tough but is the best battle I have fought as it is a battle for me, for my happiness and my wellbeing. This is by far the best prescription I've ever discovered for living a life of joy and happiness.

To put it simply, I discovered that we become what we think about, and I have the ability to choose the thoughts I allow in my life. I realized that I had to control my thoughts otherwise they would control me.

I started teaching and applying everything I was learning and working for me with my family members, with my friends, with my children, with my patients, and at times, even with strangers, and what I continue to see, every day is an incredible life developing right before my eyes. A life that I am creating. A reality that is worth living. A life where I am happy, healthy and I continue to become empowered and motivated, every day, to make a difference in others, in the same way I was able to experience this difference in my own life.

I want to scream it to the world and make sure the whole world hears that we are not our past medical or personal history but rather we can write a new prescription for a brand-new future.

We can create the script of our lives and must realize that we have total and absolute control of our future and that everything, absolutely everything we need is already within us.

We need to look in the right place for the right answers. I spent years looking outside of myself for those answers and yet found nothing. I discovered all the answers all lie within each and every one of us and that life force guides us, protects us, and inspires us to live the life of our dreams. True magic and freedom happen when we realize we have this power to change our life.

Today, I am happy, joyous, free and my life is filled with passion, purpose, and possibility. I am on a mission to impact people around the world helping them understand what it is to really live rather than simply exist.

The following words are the best dose of medicine you can ever give yourself.

I am healthy. I am happy. I live a life of prosperity and abundance. I am loved. I am magical. I am perfect. I am me.

The Courageous Queen

By Joanna Kleier

Edmund Burke said, "*The only thing necessary for the triumph of evil is for good men to do nothing*".

I was born in Burbank CA. USA on the floor in a triplex on October 17th, 1970, and I am the fifth child out of eight pregnancies. That was back in the day when women used midwives to deliver babies in their homes.

I grew up with one brother and four sisters and unfortunately my parents tragically lost my brother at the age of 7 due to complications from Lymphoma in 1966. I have to give my parents credit for persevering through a very turbulent time and pushing through till the end. Their strength and courage taught me to do the same for myself.

On the surface I was living the American Dream, but deep down I was in a nightmare, trapped in a state of autopilot as a high functioning alcoholic.

Have you ever felt like everything on the outside of your life looked entirely different that was happening on the inside? Well, that's what happened to me!

As I said, I had the American Dream, with the house, husband, two beautiful children, two dogs and my first job for 31 years but I was dying inside with low self esteem which included shame, guilt, alcohol addiction, being scared, and running away from any deep intimate relationships with those in my own family.

Rock Bottom for me started in 2014, where my addiction for alcohol had increased over time from its beginnings when I was 21 till the age of 48.

With each additional stress of adulthood piling up, I would eventually find myself out of work for five months, in bed for four and voluntarily put myself in an outpatient program for substance abuse. I was diagnosed with Major Depression and Bipolar Disorder.

Les Brown says, "*life happens for you and not to you*" and that "*a breakdown leads to a breakthrough*".

Elevation began for me after I hit my bottom and learned that I could get the help I required for recovery. Les Brown says, "*If you take responsibility for yourself, you will develop a hunger to accomplish your dreams*".

At that point I turned to outside help for healing. I've been a part of a 12-step program since 2014 and I've been able to get help for my addiction as well as help others.

They say that if you help others, it helps you and they are correct! When I achieved sobriety, approximately one year into it and attended support group meetings regularly, the clouds of despair started to lift, and I felt the rush of energy for life. I saw that I could turn the dark tunnel into a vast blue endless ocean. I've been traveling into my dream of a beautiful beachside home as I work on myself each day. Les Brown's mantra rang true for me at that time; "*If you fall, fall on your back cause If you can look up you can get up*".

Building a foundation on "Rock" for myself with self love was the next step for me in my recovering journey to wellness.

I was introduced to Danette May, a Health and Wellness Expert in 2019. This turn of events changed my life forever! Danette May wrote the book "The Rise" An Unforgettable Journey of Self Love, Forgiveness and Transformation" about her story and her rise to self love. This is a must read for women who desire to find inner peace in such a chaotic time working, raising children, running a household while trying to care for herself.

Danette May introduced me to meditation and visualization, healthy food combinations, exercises and a tribe of women supporting each other in their journey to self love. This is where the beginning of love for myself started, and it brought me out of the pit of despair and for that I am so grateful.

"*Your job is to fill your cup up, so it overflows. Then you can serve others joyfully from your saucer.*" says Lisa Nichols. I have spent the last six years working on being honest with my problems and getting help. I realize I can't help others until I take care of myself. In our past generation we have been taught that it is selfish to please oneself, but self love is not selfish!

Please take a moment every day to do self care first. Try to, meditate, pray, visualize, get into motion, and eat healthy live foods so you can live a long healthy prosperous life.

Reconnecting to oneself is key to success! Also ignoring negative people can be of great help as well.

"Don't let anyone's opinion of you become your reality" Les Brown.

Successful people only hang around quality people, and I find this to be very helpful.

Unfortunately, even family members can limit our exposure to a healthy environment at times so that we can maintain a healthy outlook on life. I suggest you find only quality people to spend your time with and if you have to remove certain people out of your life it is ok to do so.

As Mahatma Gandhi has said, *"A man is but a product of his thoughts, what he thinks he becomes".* I have been studying "Mindset, meditation and visualizations with Danette May and Fitrise 365" It has been a Life Changing Program.

I Recently found a program called "Thinking Into Results" created by Bob Proctor and Sandy Gallagher. I learned how to wake up each day and go into gratitude and learn through constant repetition of new information over and over again to shift old paradigms to new paradigms. This creates a new way of thinking. In the span of three months, I saw a great shift in my thinking from negativity to positivity. This is an awesome program and I highly recommend it for those who are struggling during these stressful times.

Thriving to achieve my dreams I never thought was possible until now! Now that I think positively, I fill my cup up with goodness and surround myself with only quality people. I can be and do whatever I desire. Les Brown says, *"Shoot for the moon and you'll land among the stars!"*

Helping people is something my parents and I have always done, and it brings me immense joy. My father had a morning ritual every morning to make his day go smoothly and I do as well. Make sure you take the necessary steps to ensure you have taken care of yourself first and remember it is not selfish to do so.

I love my daily regiment for myself of reading the self confidence formula, making a gratitude list, meditation, reading something uplifting for 30 minutes, listening to something inspirational, walking in nature and eating live foods. This has brought me great joy and a true happiness that I never had before. I truly can now say I love Joanna!

As Mahatma Gandhi says *"Live as if you were going to die tomorrow. Learn as if you were going to live forever"*.

Just because you find yourself at your bottom does not mean you can't dust yourself off and get up and start your life all over again.

There is a saying I came up with and that is when you are at your bottom there is only one way to go... Up!

I am proud to say that now I am a Certified Transformational Coach, Motivational Speaker, Author, and President of the House of Helping Hands, helping Domestic Violence Victims and last but not least a World Changer!

You will find everything you want in life! It is already there; you just have to find it. Set goals, think positively, and dream big! You are enough!!

I am very proud to be able to join in my first opportunity as an author in the "Hunger for the Hustle" book with such an elite group of men and women. Our belief in ourselves and each other is making it possible for us to help millions with our stories and our voice. We are building a legacy for all future generations to be able to pass down stories of loss, strength, perseverance, and triumph.

Bali Daze [Smiling Inside and Out]

By Susan Fowler

Sometimes the smallest of places can teach us the biggest of lessons.

I flew from London to Kuala Lumpur – my first long haul flight! I had never seen such a huge airplane, it had 2 levels and my first thought was, how could this thing actually fly? The service on board was amazing, so many films to watch, TV shows, radio... the choices were endless. I did not have any time to sleep!!!

On arrival at Kuala Lumpur, I checked into the Transit Hotel. In the middle of this huge, bustling airport, was this five-star luxury sanctuary, the view from my window looked out over the city. When I arrived, it was nighttime, and the view was amazing. I would have liked to stay there longer. Flying out of Kuala Lumpur was rather extraordinary... having reached the boarding gate there were armed police and a huge man with a microscopic lens checking passports... phew they let me on the plane, however two gentlemen were not allowed to board and were most upset. I wondered all the way to Bali where their journey ended?

I arrived in Bali and met up with my daughter Laura and we headed to our first hotel. I had never seen anywhere as beautiful and calming. In Bali they follow the Hindu religion and all statues, trees and just about anything is sacred to them. All sacred items have scarves tied around them and each day offerings of rice and flowers are left under them...all of these are symbols of good fortune and luck.

The following day we hired a jeep which had no windows, just two seats and space to put our luggage and I had a lot of luggage! In fact, it was at this point when Laura started to laugh at the sheer amount of clothes I thought I needed for 3 weeks.

Laura did all the driving and the navigating too, so I had to do was sit and take in all the scenery, from lush forests to dry beaches and quaint little villages…it was breathtaking. Now on the roads in Bali, there are no rules, or at least none that we could understand, a sound of a horn could mean anything, children ride motorbikes wearing no shoes and the roads are in places very poorly maintained. The jeep had no suspension, and this is where I began to realise that Bali was completely different to anywhere I had ever been before, and it made me smile inside and out.

As Bali is on the equator, the sun rises at 6am and sets at 6pm every day. We spent most evenings on a beach watching the sunsets as the beach comes alive with the local people gathering to worship as the sun sets by singing and playing drums. This created a beautiful soundtrack to end each day with and was quite magical to see.

One day we got up at 3am and with just two guides we climbed Mt Batur which is an active volcano. We set off at this time so that by the time we reached the summit we could watch the epic sunrise. This was one of the most physically challenging things I have ever done, the guides spoke no English, it was dark with a thick fog and very cold. The altitude made my lungs ache, but reaching the top felt amazing! It was cold, misty, and beautifully silent and peaceful at the summit. I was admiring the view when the guides introduced us to a lady called Mya who lived in a small tin hut at the top of the mountain with her cat. Much to my delight she made us some strong coffee, to help us on the rest of our journey. The guides then proceeded to cook our breakfast by putting a pan straight onto the ground and cracking eggs into it, using the heat from the volcano to cook them. I was bemused by this and again, it made me smile inside and out.

The climb down was actually harder than the climb up, as once the morning sun had risen it was very hot, humid, and dusty. We arrived back at our hotel at around 2pm and when I took my shoes off my foot had gone blue and was very bruised… strangely it did not hurt…after a very welcome cool shower I realized that my toenail had fallen off, and there was my first lesson in climbing a volcano… wear the correct shoes!

The following day we drove to the Port of Lombok. This was a long drive on very mountainous roads and would really test anyone's ability to drive. At one point Laura could not get the jeep to go into a low enough gear and we were stuck halfway up a very steep track!! We decided that I would try to get the gear changed, so we had to swap seats moving very carefully as we were not certain that the handbrake would hold the jeep in place. By some miracle we got the jeep up the hill. I felt so relieved to be at the top of the hill until we saw that the road down was just one gigantic hill going back down to the post at sea level. Driving down that hill in first gear and using both the brake pedal and handbrake to slow us down was absolutely terrifying, we reached the port somewhat traumatized and dishevelled and glad that drive was over. We left the jeep here which we were both quite glad to see the back of really and boarded a small ferry to the amazing island of Gili Trawangan.

The island was small enough to walk all the way round, the beaches were golden and totally unspoilt, it was a tranquil retreat with very few people and relaxing was easy. This island was exactly like somewhere straight out of Robinson Crusoe, and we spent a few days there swimming in the clear blue sea and jumping the huge waves.

To return to the mainland we got a classic wooden boat known as a longboat, which is actually a small boat. There were 2 crew and just 6 passengers. By this point in our journey, I had accrued a rather large number of items, ranging from wooden statues to handmade bedspreads and even had to buy a huge basket to carry them all in. As there was nowhere to put my basket, I carried it on my knees. The crossing was rough, the waves were higher than the boat and the boat took on water as it has no real roof. We sat opposite each other staring at each other, with me clinging onto my shopping as I was not having my shopping lost at sea. Laura later expressed to me that she had wondered why we had ever got on this boat which was clearly not seaworthy. I was too scared to even feel seasick. However, we did reach dry land and saw the funny side of it much later. We still laugh, to this day about me sitting there clinging onto a huge basket.

Bali maybe just a small island in Indonesia, however it has a huge place in my heart. The beaches, the forests, the culture, the sunsets, the people, all completely fascinated me and still do, to this day. The way of life there is so simple and relaxed; where less is truly more, and I feel everything is much more appreciated compared to many other parts of the world I have visited.

I have been back to Bali on two other occasions and my experiences taught me that I could do things that I never imagined I could do, whilst seeing beautiful things along the way. Even though sometimes the journey was one that tested my capabilities physically and mentally and pushed me right out of my comfort zone, it still makes me laugh today and makes me smile inside and out. If you ever get a chance, you must go to this magical place and see for yourself, so that it can bring a smile to your world inside and out.

From the Streets to Success

By Larry Normile

Have you ever been in a dark place and couldn't seem to find your way out? I've been there many times in my life, and I'd like to share with you how I got free.

My father passed away when I was 16 years old, and it spun me out of control. I didn't know how to handle it and I went into a dark place. Soon after my father passed, I dropped out of school and bounced around from friends houses just to have a place to sleep. After a while I linked up with some friends that were also in dark places. That soon caught up to me and landed me in jail at 18.

I spent the next few years sleeping on a roll out mattress on the floor with 2 other men. Both my cell mates Richard and Kevin were in jail for murder. Richard was a blessing more than he could have even imagined. He had a son that was a couple years older than me. That was also in jail for murder. Rich blamed himself for this and I believe he saw his son in me. He would talk to me everyday about goals and dreams. Most of the time I blew him off with BS goals. Then one day he sat me down and said Larry, you'll be getting out soon and I want to know your goals.

Please take a minute and think about some dreams and goals you have.

Let me explain to you why this is so important. When I was sitting in that cell, I really had a lot of time to think. So, for the next few days I really started to think about what was in my heart and soul that I really wanted to do. After a few days Rich came up to me and asked me again what my goals were. This time I had 2 goals set and I knew in all of my heart and soul these were the goals that I was going to do.

Have you ever set a goal to be something? Yet you knew nothing about the industry you wanted to be in.

That's what happened to me. My first goal was to open a tattoo studio and be known all over the world. The crazy part about this was I had only been tattooing with a sewing needle, thread and Indian ink. I had no idea about the machines artists used or even how to properly apply the ink to the skin. But I didn't let that stop me from believing that when I got out of jail, I was going to be a tattoo artist.

The second goal was to take care of my mother. When my father passed, I left my mom to grieve on her own. The day she lost my father she also lost me. That was a burden I lived with for years. I also forced my mom to claim bankruptcy because of me.

Let's fast forward 20 years later. I have been tattooing professionally now for 20+ years. I own and operate Artistic Additions Tattoo in Delaware. It has been a crazy 20 years of trials and tribulations, but I never gave up on my goals. The best part of tattooing for me is getting to hear the reason behind wanting a tattoo and me getting to tell the story for you, with art. I have been blessed to travel all over the world to tattoo and have met some amazing souls.

My second goal was reached in March of 2020. I was blessed to be able to buy my mothers house, pay off all her debt and remodel her house for her. My mother has been my rock and crutch in my life whenever I needed her, and this was my way of saying thank you for everything you've done and continue to do for me. I love you mom.

Now that I hit my goals, I set over 20 years ago, I realized I needed some new ones. The only difference between these goals and the ones I set 20 years ago, is the fact I understand how powerful my mindset and energy are to my goals.

My new goals are: To be on TV, to build the Amazon of tattoo supplies, write a book, to produce my documentary, to help my children find their passion in life and to take Next Generation Outcome worldwide and teach as many lost souls as possible, the power of mindset and energy. I set these goals in May of 2020. Now let me take you on the journey of what has happened since I set these goals.

I was honored and blessed to be one of the first top 20 speakers in Les Browns Power Summit. I believe my story needed to be heard so the little Larry's would be able to relate. Thank you Les, for everything you've done for me.

I decided one day that I needed a coach to help me navigate in my mindset and business. Little did I understand the power of this at the time. So, I reached out to Jon Talarico, he is the number one wealth and business coach in Bob Proctors 'Thinking into Results' program. Jon and I had a 15 min phone call that turned into an hour-long conversation. I felt he understood me, and I understood him. That was the beginning of a great friendship.

After Jon worked with me for a couple weeks, he started helping me find my way. He linked me up with Spike Van Briesen. He is an amazing producer of Reality TV. With hits like 'The Hills' and 'The X Factor', to his most recent one, 'Gordon Ramsay's 24 hours to Hell and Back'. Spike and I meet every Wednesday to work on my pitch deck for my TV show. Thank you Spike, for helping me understand more about this industry. Congratulations on the big promotion, you deserve it. You are one of the most humble and pure souls I've had the honor to meet.

I am a month or so out from finishing my book called 'Billionaire Mindset'. It is a book about all the mindsets it took for me to get to where I am today.

I have been filming my documentary to becoming a billionaire. The best part about this is my son and his company are the ones filming the documentary.

I have recently linked up with another amazing soul. He has helped me get to the point now that I am buying tattoo supply companies to build the Amazon of tattoo supply stores.

Last but not least, Next Generation Outcomes is a non-profit Organization that works with troubled and lost youth to help them find their passion and the right mindset for success. Our goal with this Organization is to be worldwide and help the little Larry's find their way. So far, we have been to local prisons and schools and have had the opportunity to help the ones wanting the help. Now in 2021 we are expanding our reach. Thanks to Vanity for putting me in contact with the right person to help me with this.

I know you're probably wondering what this has to do with you. It has everything to do with you.

I am a high school drop out that statically shouldn't have what I have. The reason I do have what I have is because I used everything in my past as a lesson learned. I also have come to realize with the right mindset, any goal you want to achieve, can be achieved.

In the words of one the BEST speakers to ever speak, Les Brown - *"Shoot for the Moon, so even if you miss you are amongst the stars"*. That is more than just a quote, that is a fact. If you would've told me 20 years ago, I'd be where I am today, I would've laughed. Now if I say I will be or do something I know I can and I will.

I want to take this time to thank Michael, Jake, and everyone behind the scenes for making this book possible. It is an honor to be apart of something that is going to help change lives. You guys are amazing human beings and the skies the limit for you.

The Far Country

By Kasundra "Dr. K." Brown

I wake up every morning excited to start the new day. I know everything will not go as planned. There will be hiccups, missed deadlines, or someone's poor planning will create an emergency for me. In other words, life will happen. But I am ready for whatever comes. I know I can choose how to respond and not just go along to get along with everyone else's wants and even needs. It was not always this way. Prior to my marriage I was a bold, exciting, somewhat opinionated, and confident single mom of one. I knew what I wanted, when and how I wanted it and more importantly, from where and how to get it. Immediately after divorce, I was a wounded, depressed, unsure of myself, single again, mom of four. It was a struggle to say the least to get back to the place I now call home, owning my identity, and accepting my true self.

My mother was the only person who did not think my ex-husband and I were "right for each other." All our friends thought we made a "cute couple" - we were both in our thirties, gainfully employed, never married, and mature. Each of us brought a child into the relationship. Wild oats had been sown, harvests reaped, and we were both ready to settle down and raise our sons in a two-parent nuclear family. We agreed there would be no step-kids or stepparents in our house; we all belonged to each other.

However, my mom saw traits in him that she did not like and made every effort to warn me about. She noticed the cultural differences between a woman from north Texas, raised to be independent and a man from the West Indies who was raised in a traditional, conservative home. She knew that he would want a typical, passive wife who catered to his every desire and that he would not appreciate a woman who had her own mind and did not want to be anybody's "step and fetch it." So, this marriage was destined to have major problems from the beginning. What she could not warn me about, was both our insecurities which caused him to be very needy and me to become the very thing I had vowed I would never be. The funny thing is, it all started while we were dating, and I wasn't even aware of it.

When my ex and I began dating and I let him know that I enjoyed going to movies, he informed me that he did not like movie theatres because "Someone will be sick, and sneeze or cough and I'll catch a deadly, incurable disease." Did I say he was a bit of a hypochondriac? For this reason alone, I never took him to see "Contagion." What I later learned is that he did not like going anywhere where people were present. His idea of a nice date was a night in, watching tv or an afternoon of doing what became our favorite past time, working on cars; well, he would work on cars, and I would keep him company. If I wanted to go to the movies or do anything else that involved people, I went with my son or with a friend, but not with him. This went on for some years as we dated on and off during our almost decade long friendship prior to becoming man and wife.

Once married, I gave up going to movies all together. I can't tell you exactly when it happened. During our marriage, we saw two theatre movies at my insistence. We sat against the back wall to calm his nerves, even though I enjoyed sitting in the center. He talked throughout both movies. Every time someone cleared their throat, coughed, or sneezed, "Kas do you think they have anything I can catch?" "My throat is itching, I musta caught whatever that body has." "Have you seen enough? Are you ready to go now?" Theatres became such an unpleasant experience with him that I never asked to go again, not even to see musicals which I loved. This became the case pretty much wherever we went, so we did not go out often.

As it became clear that our marriage was going to end, I started seeing a psychologist. During one of our sessions, she asked "What do you like to do?" Believe it or not, that was a revelatory question. We were discussing how I could rebuild my life since moving out of my house and filing for divorce. I mentioned that I felt like I had lost my identity in the ten years I was married to my ex. By that time, we had four sons: two adults and two in elementary school. Everything I did seemed to be for the benefit or enjoyment of someone else. I hadn't done anything for my own personal pleasure in years. My youngest son was an extreme preemie born four months ahead of schedule. Once he came home from the hospital, there were doctors' appointments, hospitalizations, early intervention, and therapy. The older boys were into sports, band, music lessons, Civil Air Patrol and working after school and on the weekends. Son number 3, just two years older than his baby brother, needed to be potty trained, hugged, held, and read to as well as go on trips to the park and playgroups so that he could maintain appropriate socialization and stimulation for a child his age. Then there was my husband who had his own "special" set of needs. For ten years, I was so busy meeting everyone else's needs and making sure they had as much of what they wanted as possible that I stopped thinking about and pursuing what I needed or wanted outside of the necessities of life; food, clothing, and shelter.

In a later session with my psychologist, I was asked a question. My immediate answer was, "I'm not sure." She asked, "What did you enjoy doing before you were married?" I thought for what seemed like forever and suddenly blurted out "I loved going to the movies." "Do you still go to the movies?" she asked. "No." I said. "What stopped you?" she asked. I said, "What do you mean what stopped me?" "You said you loved going to the movies before you got married. I asked do you still go to the movies, and you said no. So, what stopped you from going to the movies since it is something that you enjoy." I answered, "My husband doesn't like going to movies because he thinks someone will cough or sneeze and he will catch some deadly, incurable disease." Her response, "Thank you for telling me why your husband doesn't go to movies, but I asked why you don't go to movies." "I told you", and I repeated the answer I had just given. To which she replied, "Again, thank you for telling me why your husband doesn't go to movies. Now, please tell me why YOU don't go to movies." This went on for three or four more rounds. Each time I became more exasperated in my response. It really was a sight. She remained calm with each inquiry, while I repeatedly said with growing annoyance, "Because my husband doesn't like to go to the movies. He's afraid someone will ..."

I stopped mid-sentence as the light dawned in the marble hallway of my mind. I finally got it. Only then did she ask a different question. "Did he ask you to stop going?" "No." I said. "Did he demand it of you? If you chose to go to the movies with one of your girlfriends, do you think he would have forbidden it?" "Oh! No way in hell would he dare tell me what I couldn't do." was my offended response. "So why did you stop doing what you enjoy?" "I, I stopped going" I stammered. She said, "Right. That's it. You stopped. You gave up yourself. No one took you from you. You relinquished you voluntarily." I realized at that moment that my identity had not been lost or stolen; I had freely sent it away. By not taking the time to do the things I enjoyed, I chose not to practice good self-care and in the course of time lost touch with my true self. "The good news," my therapist said with a smile, "is that you still have you and what you have freely surrendered you can now reclaim. The next time we meet, I want you to tell me what you did just because you wanted to do it."

I left her office feeling like a voyager returning home from a long trip to a foreign land. Home was now the unfamiliar territory and the far country had become the place where I was most at ease. We discovered several other areas where I had let go of myself and given others the right to rule me. It was hard work breaking the habit of answering simple questions like "What do you want to eat" with "I don't care, you choose." Or "What do you want to do tonight" with "It doesn't matter, you decide." I learned, as I honestly answered each of those seemingly trivial questions, that I moved closer and closer to the real me, eventually giving myself permission to freely express my wants and needs and to have them met. I also developed the discipline of reflecting on each day and sometimes individual events by asking myself, "Were you true to yourself today?" "Did you bring your authentic self to the table?" I congratulated myself each time I truthfully answered "Yes." When the answer was "No" I'd tell myself, "Be careful to be more honest tomorrow."

I do not remember exactly what I did the week my therapist gave me the assignment to do something just because I wanted to. I do know that 13 years later it is still a regular habit. A whole new world opened for me when I came back to myself from the far country of pleasing others. It will for you too, if you will be truly honest about what you want and need when you have the opportunity to choose.

Kasundra "Dr. K." Brown is a motivational teacher, speaker, author, and transformative thought coach who specializes in the practical application of Biblical TRUTH and Universal LAW. To engage her services, email doctork@theyiltedfedoratrainer.net To learn more from her, follow her on Facebook @FedoraOnTilt and or join her Thursday Night Bible study, @ConnectingtheDotsBibleStudy. You may also subscribe to her YouTube channel, Kasundra Brown Speaks and visit her websites:

thetiltedfedoratrainer.net[23] and krbrownministries.org[24]

---

23. http://thetiltedfedoratrainer.net
24. http://www.krbrownministries.org/

Re-Built and Brilliant

By Wayne Johnson

The most freeing words that have ever left my mouth… "I QUIT!"

What I wasn't prepared for was how hard I had to crash in order to rise into my greatness.

I felt frozen in a job, working for someone else; being told what to do and how to do it, when I knew that I could handle the tasks without someone giving me directives, so I quit! What next?

Well, I thought it couldn't be that hard to choose a venture and find a niche to start my own business. That was my plan of action. Hey, there would be money in the bank, and no one to answer to; as easy as that. Well, I pursued my desire, only to discover how wrong I was!

Little did I know that being your own boss came with many responsibilities: Rota's, payroll, working day and night. You name it, I do it all. From my experience, it is not half as easy as it looks and sounds. Many who are employed by a company have the notion that someone who owns a business, has all the time in the world and a bank full of cash. When someone owns a business, they must pass through lots of red tape and overcome obstacles before that statement is even partially true.

The first successful business that I started was a Vehicle Rental Company, in the overspill car park at the side of a beauty salon; (which I already part owned with my beautiful sister, Claire.) I decided to name the company, **Mental Rental;** (supporting slogan) **A Mental Rate for Your Rental Mate**. I gave it that catchy name phrase so that it would stick in people's minds; the idea stemmed from a joke with a good friend. The starting process was quick. I bought a few vans, got them insured, and hired them out; then things started to get complicated. There were issues with drivers, licenses, parking tickets, speeding tickets, damaged vehicles, finance companies, bad debt; the list was endless. Was I aware of how much vehicle hire really entailed? NO!

I started out with all pre-owned vans. I then gradually moved from just vans to cars, and then to minibuses, all types of vehicles for hire. I then branched out even more to relate with the social trends at the time and brought a party bus and gyroscope which we took to Croatia along with our team. As my business grew, I became open to more opportunities, and became more knowledgeable of the depth of the industry I was working with. We became part of a rental network and became privy to other ways of accessing and funding vehicles. We then progressed from pre-owned vehicles to brand new vehicles. We started to outgrow the premises we were then leasing. It was time for us to move, so we bought a bigger place, and business started to boom in such a way that I had to employ more staff.

Within six months, my business was scaling new heights. We got to a position where at times all the vehicles were rented; we did not have enough vehicles to supply our customers. The demand was more than the supply, I felt accomplished. We we're 12 months and the business was doing great; after some thorough revision, a lengthy application and a dragon's den style interview I was given the best opportunity so far within my growing business education. I was selected to be among the elite, Goldman Sachs 10,000 Small Businesses growth Programme. I never dreamt that my business would land me in such a place. Having this status opened a new world of knowledge in other aspects of businesses; some of which I was not acquainted with before. I got connected with people who were working in other industries, and they opened my eyes to a new world of business education. Seeing where I was coming from, this experience made me feel elated; I was just a humble fellow coming from a low socio-economic background, with not much education.

As business continued the upward path, I purchased my dream car and different levels of clientele entered my business, I started to make way for high-end cars. They soon came flooding in and we started bursting at the seams. Due to this, we had to branch out again, and purchase more premises to accommodate the influx of new business. Now with this heavy inflow, I had to hire new employees; this was now a whole different ball game. Connection with myself, other people, my surroundings, and thoughts all began to change. My life began to spiral into a whole new world. In a short space of time, vehicle after vehicle was being funded via my main business. After a while prestige attracted a wider range of clientele. With many of these clients, vehicles were being returned damaged, bills were not paid, and we had to chase customers to pay their bills; (customers had to leave a deposit to hire a vehicle but if it was later returned damaged, they could not afford their final bill, meaning we had to take customers down the legal route e.g., CCJ). Consequently, my company started to feel the brunt financially. With income dropping, my vehicle hire company started to struggle. My once 'successful' business began to plummet. It was on a never-ending downward spiral.

When my business model changed from vans to cars, the whole concept of the business had changed. I soon found out that when it came to selling cars as apposed to vans the model was different. When you sell a commercial vehicle, its generally sold plus VAT (the value-added tax). However, it was a different ball game when it came to selling cars as they would be sold inclusive of VAT leaving me with a 20% short fall on the cash position on every car sold, unless sold to a VAT Registered Business. I felt like I was getting in the ring with Mike Tyson everyday getting hit with early repayment charges for settling vehicles in fixed contracts early and depreciation across all 170 vehicles was affecting us across the board. It then became a game of robbing Peter to pay Paul not a good business model.

The business was then in a financial tailspin. I was chasing delinquent debtors without success. I lost my properties and my dream car. I was truly feeling trapped. I had to eventually employ a financial advisor for the number side of things and tried to offload as many vehicles as I could, to input cash back into the company.

It seemed like a financial nightmare, what I had put my life, heart, and soul into for the past 10 years was being pulled from right beneath my feet, and I fell into a dark hole. We had to go into administration (the company closed, and all assets were liquidated.) With money low and struggling to provide for my loved ones the way I was used to, I became disconsolate.

I started reading motivational literature and focusing on everything I taught myself, (things they do not teach you in the education system/school.) Les Brown, Brian Tracy, Myles Munroe & Jim Rohn (I still study these authors and thought leaders today and I suggest you do too) and was introduced to similar videos. I was feeling defeated, but the motivational videos and literature gave me hope.

I learnt that readers are leaders and learners are earners.

I found that I had greatness in me, and that I was a winner. They we're things that despite my circumstances no one could ever take away from me. All of this from focusing on my personal development. I cannot preach this enough to everyone. Take some time to invest in yourself it will be one of the best investments you ever make.

2019 the start of a new beginning. Soon after consistently listening to the motivational videos, one of the first customers that I had in my first business, approached me with a new opportunity (A joinery business). This was a different industry; a totally new field, but I was happy to welcome it, put my shoulder to the wheel and give it my best shot. I learned my role in the business, invested in my education concerning the intricacies of this niche. I then sought to level up to my opponents, by researching the gaps in this industry and filling them with much needed value. The investment and hard work paid off, and I am so glad they did! I feel I am back on track with financial freedom, and I am able to take care of my family and my responsibilities once again with ease and comfort.

I made use of my original vehicles, original resources, and of course kept my hardworking employees with me (one of which being my niece, Tyler who has been with me since she left school); along with the knowledge of our previous failure (which by now I had come to realise had brought me some great perspective and value) and a whole new growing team of experienced craftsmen and builders. We operate out of our factory in the heart of Birmingham, and I truly believe we provide quality service that delivers confidence, value and peace of mind.

All our projects are designed and created by some of the finest craftsman, who are passionate about their work and pride themselves on being able to provide clients with the same uncompromising standards. I now have my own reliable building team; the knowledge and the skill set to focus on one of my new goals of becoming a property developer within the next 12 months.

We are the Transform Group, transforming your vision into reality.

thetransformgroup.co.uk[25]

Throughout the years, whilst carrying out building works, I discovered that the majority of residential and commercial properties that we were renovating or demolishing had many reusable building materials being taken to landfill, thus giving me the idea of advertising them for sale to see if there was a market for reclaimed materials, from this Birmingham Reclaimed was born and it was a success.

We started out by specialising in the reclamation of Timbers, Plywood's, Bricks and most other building materials, our everyday car boot sale. Working in partnership with my building company 'The Transform Group', we have been able to help customers with a lower budget afford to achieve their dream home or project by using recycled materials and keeping the costs low, especially after the way the world has been over the past few years.

Since 2020 we have recycled 240,000 lengths of timber and 55,000 plywood's and we are only just beginning.

'Birmingham Reclaimed,' Reduce Reuse Recycle We now focus on selling new and used building materials to trade and the public and with the state of the current environment, we continue to do our best to contribute to the sustainability of our planet.

Linktr.ee/Birminghamreclaimed

---

25. http://www.thetransformgroup.co.uk

I am yet to tell you the full story behind this industry but let me live through it a little first. What I can tell you though, is that my businesses The Transform Group and Birmingham Reclaimed; Are on the upswing; I am feeling successful once more and ready to take on the world.

4 years ago, I never knew how to use a tape measure correctly, I knew everything about cars and vans but nothing about building works. I now have a successful building company and reclamation yard. I have gained the knowledge to switch from imperial to metric measurements in the matter of seconds and add great value to each of my customers. If you asked me 5 years ago where I would be now, this is not what I would have predicted! I now know that the meaning of being successful isn't having the dream car but it is having successful business', healthy family, many holidays throughout the year and good mental health.

Thank you so much for taking time to read this chapter. I would like to thank my mother Shirley for being my rock. My beautiful wife to be Kara for all the support she has given me over the years through thick and thin, she has been my biggest fan. Most importantly blessed me with two beautiful sons Giorgio and Emilio; these 3 are my world. I would lastly like to say a special thankyou to Mike Johnson, (not my biological father but lucky enough to share our surnames;) he has been my business guide, mentor and a friend that has become family. To all the people who have helped me along the way, from my heart and soul I am truly grateful, Thank You.

'When life knocks you down, make sure you land on your back. Because if you can look up, you can get up - Les Brown'

The Secret of Happiness

By Denise Nicholson

My mother suddenly disappeared when I was three years old. I looked everywhere but couldn't find her. Whenever I asked my relatives for her, they always responded, "She'll come home soon." I spent days looking out the windows, waiting for her to come home. Sometimes, I walked around the house looking for her in the places she'd hidden when we played Hide-and-seek—still, no sight of her.

I was born in Jamaica, West Indies, in 1972. I lived in the hills of Sligoville, St. Catherine, with my mother and father, four siblings, and my grandparents. When I was born, migrating to England or America from the islands was typical for young adults seeking work or seeking better opportunities for themselves and their children. When the chance came for the parent, they would leave their children with an acceptable adult. The parents could now go to the foreign country to work for a while, save money and return home.

My mother was among the herd of young people who were smitten enough to travel abroad to pursue opportunities. She went to America in search of work, leaving her five children behind. It was just only a few weeks after my mother's "disappearance" that my father died. My grandmother told me he died in a car accident, and he was never coming back. Although this was an unexpected event, I didn't look for him when he didn't wake me up for morning walks before breakfast. It didn't worry me that he didn't come to find me to play or walk with him to get fruits and vegetables from his farm. There was a big Nine-night celebration for him, and I, along with my siblings, ate, sang, and danced the night away with the mourners. At the end of the celebrations, my father was buried in a grave in his parents' backyard.

Almost immediately after my father's death, my great-grandmother from out of town came to visit and took me when she left. Thus, my "foster child" experiences began. I went from home to home; by the time I was six years old, I had already lived in four different family members' homes.

By this time, I understood that my mother had gone to America, or "farin," as Jamaicans say. My days were cheerful, but I spent my nights dreaming of seeing my mother again. When I became a teenager, I traveled by myself to the country to visit my siblings and grandparents. While visiting one weekend, my aunt came to take me back to Kingston. She hung her head as I walked up to her. With tears welled up in her almond-shaped eyes, she mumbled, "Mom is dead." I had no idea whose mom she was talking about, but by her appearance, I knew it must be important, so I asked, "Who died?" Her mouth trembled as she lifted her voice and was direct. "Your mother died," she stuttered. "How!" I screamed. "In a horrible car accident." The news came so heavy and painful; I couldn't believe it. I spent years praying and hoping to see my mother again, only to see my anticipation taken away abruptly. Just like my mother, my hopes died. I fainted. My siblings and I were crushed; we mourned the disappearance of the opportunity ever to see our mother again.

My aunt lifted my body unto hers, hugged me, and whispered, "I know it hurts, but pull yourself together. You must be stronger now than you've ever been. Look at your brothers and sister; they need you." I looked around the room but could barely see out of my swollen eyes. I nonetheless saw the look of hopelessness and despair in their dispositions. "We have to go and prepare for the embassy; you all need visas so you can go to America for her funeral." My aunt said. I restrained my disappointment and anger and saw the hope of going to the United States.

When we arrived in the United States, my mother was already buried. While living in the United States, my mother had four additional children, so now there were nine of us. We all lived with one of my mothers' sisters and her family. At fifteen years old, I had the audacity of becoming sexually active, and of course, I got pregnant. And then I was asked to leave my aunt's home.

My boyfriend's family invited me to live with them, and we did for a few months. Before my baby was born, we moved to our apartment. Having to take care of a family, a home, and going to high school was more responsibility than my teenage boyfriend, and I could have ever imagined. We were not equipped to manage these responsibilities, and we struggled and raged through them. Mentally, it was strenuous, but I graduated from high school and then studied Cosmetology. After beauty school, I opened a salon, had my daughter, and got married to the same guy.

At the beauty salon, I was happy. I enjoyed my client's interactions, and I loved hearing their stories, struggles, and successes. But at home, I moped around in my bathrobe and uncombed hair and barely smiled. The weight of our issues was hard to bear, and we argued regularly. Considering how I was feeling, I wasn't surprised when I was diagnosed with depression. I fantasized about not waking up ever or driving my minivan over a bridge. One day, after another argument, I found myself crying and pacing in the backyard, pondering whether to pick up rocks to throw at my husband, who was inside of the house, yelling to me, "Yu can't sweep up the backyard?" Just those words made me cry hysterically; I was disconsolate, and I found myself thinking, *it is time to get out of this marriage*. I was ready for the emotional anguish to end. I then called my pastor and declared, "Pastor, I think I'm losing my mind." He immediately prayed with me and scheduled a meeting.

Meeting with my pastor engendered a paradigm shift. I complained about everything and everyone. "Him don't like mi, and mi no like him." At first, Pastor listened. Then he told me if I wanted to be happy, I needed to do three things: I must let go of all the hurt and pain, forgive myself for the mistakes I'd made, and forgive those who had hurt me. The pastor reminded me that God loved me, and even though I was hurting, God was still in charge of my life. He suggested that I plan for the life I wanted and recommended that my husband and I participate in marriage counseling before seeking to end an unhappy marriage safely.

Over the years, I've learned that being happy is a choice. Of course, societal conditions help to create an atmosphere of lack or one of fulfillment. When we are at our best; or feel safe, supported, and understood, these conditions contribute to our state of mind and our decision to be happy. However, our happiness depends on our habitual thoughts and the feelings we attach to our experiences. Despite what we experience, human beings are resilient, and we can overcome any experience if we choose to be happy.

My happiness began when I decided to pursue a nursing degree. My self-confidence increased with each "A" I earned. Eventually, my husband and I started visiting a marriage counselor, and my perceptions of myself and our marriage shifted. I became less bothered by the things he said and paid more attention to practicing positive thinking and developing my mind. Because my environment made the resources needed available and affordable, shifting my mindset to happiness was challenging but possible. Changes didn't occur immediately or suddenly; I changed my thought processes, actions, and reactions, which improved my situation.

Your happiness is your responsibility. You can't change others, but you can improve and make changes in yourself: get smarter, get stronger, get wiser. I became a registered nurse, then a nurse practitioner, who earned a doctoral degree. Now, I own a successful publishing company that helps individuals make their dreams come true.

So, based on my experiences, I have penned five golden rules to achieve happiness:

1. Develop a growth mindset; for experiences to change, your outlook must change.

2. Utilize a positive perspective; as a child, I thought my mother abandoned me. Now I say my mother left my siblings and me to create better opportunities for us all.

3. Forgive yourself and others; actions from the past should be learning experiences for the present. Learn from them and move forward.

4. Don't take things personally; people will be who they are and make decisions based on their life experiences.

5. Be humble; seek help when you feel overwhelmed. I reached out to my pastor, which saved my life and my marriage.

Our most significant source of happiness lies in the success of our relationships with those around us. We control our thoughts about them and decide the emotions we attach to these thoughts. Therefore, give others the benefit of a favorable thought.

Despite the challenges of my life experiences, it was my choice to make the changes necessary to improve my life and, ultimately, my conscious decision to have a happy life.

If you would like a free mindset assessment or feel you have a story in you and need help getting it out of your head and onto paper, I can help you get a growth mindset, become an author, and monetize your message so you can make a six-figure income and begin to live the life of your dreams. Maybe you're thinking of starting a blog and need some assistance with your content, reach out to me as I would be happy to help you take your next steps to achieving success and happiness! Schedule a call with me at denisenicholson.com[26].

---

26. https://denisenicholson.com

The Struggle is Real, But so is Your Greatness

By Barry Overton

We are all familiar with the term 'the struggle is real'. A term that embodies the thought that life is hard. Life is going to knock us down. Life will not be easy. We are quick to believe in the struggle. There are even some that would rather believe in the struggle than believe in their own victory. And while I will agree that, yes, the struggle is real. I also believe emphatically that we all have greatness within us. So, yes, the struggle is real, but so is your greatness. And it really comes down to which phrase are you going to believe in more. How will you choose to live your life?

From early childhood, struggle introduced itself to me. Growing up in the projects for a short period of time and experiencing a year of homelessness. My mom and I moved from one relative's house to another. In second grade I attended three different schools that one school year. At the age of seven years old, I didn't realize that it was homelessness I was experiencing, but I knew that it wasn't the norm. As I think back on that timeframe in my life, I realize the resiliency of humans. While my mother struggled through that time, she always made sure that I was taken care of and we had a roof over our head, even if it was someone else's roof.

It's often said that we are a product of our environment. For most of my childhood, the environment that I grew up in was Section 8 housing, food stamps, and just getting by. But it was also watching my mother who was driven to be successful in whatever she put her mind to. She was able to start a modest housekeeping business. The environment also taught me that what you set your mind to, you can achieve.

As a kid it was not a dream life, but my situation did not keep me from dreaming. Growing up in Austin, Texas in the '70s and '80s, my role models were stars on TV. One of my favorites was Superman. At a young age, I thought that I could be Superman. As I got older, I realized that the dreams of being the Superman that I saw on the big screen and on television would not necessarily be the route that I would be able to go, but there was another Superman in my life, my uncle, Freddie Maxwell. He was the first black Sergeant, Lieutenant, and Captain of the Austin Police Department. He was well admired throughout the Austin community and as his nephew, I was extremely proud of him. He was my role model.

So, prior to reaching adulthood, I realized that I too would follow the footsteps of my uncle in becoming a police officer. Initially, I saw it as a way out of poverty. I wanted a better life as an adult. I was driven to be successful. I believed in my ability to be able to do it only because I had evidence in my own family. I created a plan around it. The plan consisted of joining the military at the age of 18 as a military police officer and spending three years there gaining experience in law enforcement, while also going to college and studying criminal justice. After three years, I would be 21, at which point I could be hired on by civilian police departments.

I followed that exact plan. During my time in the military, I served as a Sergeant during the Persian Gulf War. After serving for my country, I then went on to two police departments, one in Anniston, Alabama, and another in Denver, Colorado, where I spent 26 years in law enforcement, serving my community. During those years as a police officer, I worked primarily as a narcotics detective where I received opportunities to even be deputized by the Drug Enforcement Administration. So, I had dual positions of a city police officer with the Denver Police Department, but also being deputized as a DEA Federal Task Force Officer.

During my time as a police officer, I started to experience this burning desire inside. I had a passion for business and entrepreneurship. I indulged in many different business opportunities and investment opportunities. From growing up and playing many different sports, there was a competitive nature in me. Being in business and succeeding in business fueled the competitiveness that was inside. Not only did I enjoy the success, I enjoyed the ability to be able to help other people have success.

For many years, I held dual commitments to my job as a police officer and to my business ventures. While it was a challenge, more importantly for me, it was safe. You see, the fear that I had was walking away from a six-figure income as a police officer and failing in business and losing everything. So, for 12 years, I did both. I would be the first to tell you that it's hard to give 120% at anything, but it's even harder when you're splitting it with multiple tasks that you're trying to accomplish. And trying to be a police officer as well as an entrepreneur and balance the two along with having a family was not an ideal situation for creating exponential success.

After starting a new successful business in 2012, by late 2013, I decided to walk away from that six-figure income and put all my eggs into the entrepreneur basket. I finally gained the courage to believe that my success was inevitable, and I was holding myself back by working this job that took 60 to 70 hours of my week. Steve Harvey often talks about you must leap from the cliff to find success and that you're going to hit some rocks along the way, but eventually you will soar. And I can tell you, I leaped from that cliff to find success. In the beginning, I did soar. I was flying high. Entrepreneurship was everything that I had hoped it would be.

Then came 2016. During that time, I think I hit every jagged rock that cliff had to offer. The business that had me on cloud 9 was suddenly on a downward spiral that negatively affected my income tremendously, cutting it more than in half. The financial woes started to mount up with missed credit card payments, car payments, and I was barely able to keep a roof over my head. That biggest fear that I had of leaving the police department was now a reality. But the difference is because of the personal development training that I had going into 2016, I didn't fear what was happening to me at this time.

Willie Jolley is often quoted as saying, "A setback is a setup for a comeback." In 2016, that quote became my mantra. The fear that I had years before of failing and not being able to recover was no longer a part of my thinking. Based off of the teachings of Napoleon Hill, Les Brown, Tony Robbins, and Bob Proctor, I had developed a new mindset. I embraced the struggle because I believed in my greatness. In the moment that I was going through the hardest time in my adult life, I knew that someday I would be telling this story and it would inspire others in their life. In basketball, there is a move called the pivot, where you change the direction that you were currently going. to be able to move in another direction. Life requires pivot.

In business, I realized that I was remarkably good at building relationships and gaining trust. I was a big believer in the importance of customer service. And I became a master of the pivot. So, while my current business began to fail, it didn't mean that I had to fail. At this point, in 2016, I had 15 years as a real estate agent, but in those 15 years, it was always a side hustle. It was never the main thing. But at the end of 2016, I decided to make the pivot of a lifetime to rebuild my income.

Belief, planning, and execution are the first three rungs on the ladder of success. I believed in myself. And knowing that I could be successful in the things that I put my mind to, a plan was formulated to work with some of the absolute best in the Denver market in real estate. And execution was probably the easiest for me because of my driven mentality. It led me on an upward trajectory of going from six figures a year to six figures a quarter. Even during a pandemic, when some agent's business began to suffer, I was able to practically 10X my income in 4 years. My story is not rare, it serves as an example of what's possible. I don't say this to impress you, but to impress upon you, we all have experienced struggle, but we all can also experience greatness!

So yes, the struggle is real, but so is your greatness!

A Million to Zero and Back Again in 365 Days

By Catherine Molloy

Research tells us there are two reasons we do things – either through inspiration or desperation. The interesting thing is inspiration doesn't always lead to action!

I stepped onto the main stage as thousands of new faces stared at me. My high heels tapped a confident rhythm as I walked towards the center of the stage. There is something special in the way thousands of strangers can connect so personally in one room. You see, I am driven with a crazy passion to create, support and encourage conscious leaders in this world and it's always a privilege to be on those stages.

Because only a few short months before this moment I found myself sitting at the edge of my bed, feeling desperate, face in my hands, wondering how we'd lost our million-dollar fortune.

And, as the great Holocaust survivor Viktor Frankl taught us, *"When we are no longer able to change a situation, we are challenged to change ourselves."*[3] And that's exactly what I had to do. Through desperation I had to inspire myself to choose to make a difference. If I can do this, so can you.

What I didn't do that day on stage, was share my personal journey, I wasn't ready. It was a conscious decision not to share it back then but today, with you, I'm making a different choice: this time I'm ready to share my story.

It was only recently that I realized many people on the speaking circuit and in the audience only saw me as successful. They knew my book *The Million Dollar Handshake* or saw me on stage and assumed that it was just one success after another, and I had some sort of golden secret.

But you and I know that's not the truth.

The truth is, it was hard work, steep learning curves and hustle. But yes, there is some golden secrets—and that's what I would like to share with you: the true secrets that created *all* of my success. Are you ready?

The Crisis, The Collapse, and the Conquering

In 2008 the Global Financial Crisis hit. Those three innocuous letters, "GFC" upended my life, pouring the contents of my beautiful existence onto the ground in ruins.

After it roared through my life, my husband John and I were swamped in debt. One million dollars of our hard-earned money literally disappeared in a blink. It was time to hustle and hustle hard.

Hustling wasn't entirely new to me. I had started my working career in service for the corporate banking sector and became deeply involved in learning about body language and its influence on people. Applying this, *"how may I serve you?"* philosophy wasn't just a sales technique either, it was a true, caring intention that I held for every customer I worked with.

Now, as I mentioned before, I was used to a bit of hustle. I worked in between three pregnancies but had found that the practicalities of stopping and starting work again were a little too much. So, I decided to utilize our family house as a home office and became essentially a one-stop-shop running three businesses that all complemented one another: children's books, toys and clothes. Genius, I know!

Then glandular fever decided to jump into my body and slow me right down. As the American activist Maya Angelou said, *"Nothing works until you do."* I chose not to listen to my body's signals and kept on keeping on. Over time, I ended up with four autoimmune diseases: Yikes! I hadn't been expecting all that. Have you ever had that experience where in retrospect all the signs were there, you just chose not to listen in the present moment?

The doctor looked at me seriously one day and asked, *"How do you get up in the mornings?"*

"Well," I replied, *"I get one leg out of bed, then I get the other one out, and then I'm up. I have a young family you know; I have to get up."*

Then, like the evil villain in a movie, the Global Financial Crisis struck and spiraled the global economy out of control. The housing market collapsed in the United States and triggered a downfall across the globe, including our real-estate business and personal investments. At first, we just met the crisis head-on. Nothing lasts forever, right? Maybe we could just work harder, longer, faster—right? Wrong.

I soon discovered that it's not just finances that a GFC kills; it collapses people and destroys their livelihoods and dreams.

And that's what it did to us.

One "normal" morning at home, I went into our bedroom to chat with my husband John. He wasn't out of bed yet and at first, I couldn't see him, but when I did—it marked me forever. John was curled up, his face contorted in emotional agony. I could barely hear him as he murmured, "*I just can't go back to work.*"

It was surreal yet I intuitively knew he just didn't mean he couldn't go back to work that day, he meant he could not go back to work: *period*. I had one hand on his shoulder and one part of my brain in crisis management.

Any crisis has three major parts:

Pre-crisis: preparation and prevention

Crisis response: management to respond to the crisis at hand

Post crisis: preparing for future crises with good planning and strategies

Ironically, John and I did have both a "pre-crisis plan" and a "crisis response plan" — we would run our real estate rent-roll together until the crisis was over. But John skipped the pre-crisis preparation and went headfirst into crisis, and for this particular crisis - I was also thrust headfirst into control and management.

The economy was plunging into a recession. I had to quickly learn the ropes of my husband's business.

Within a few weeks I soon found out that the working culture was dismal and there were a lot of staff issues around blame and other grievances. The salespeople weren't following through and our relationships with buyers needed some nurturing and improved processes. I couldn't go to John for help, so it was sink or swim. I decided to start paddling fast. After being there 4 weeks, I sold 3 houses on one day and 5 in a week, it was a record for the 20-year-old company. I wanted to keep the business. One of my learnings was every skill we have is transferable, all we need is within us already, we just need to believe in ourselves and of course desperation was my driver though inspiration for a better future had now taken over.

The GFC was still impacting our financial state and with it, John's mental wellbeing. John looked at me one day and admitted honestly, *"Cath, I won't get better while we have the real estate business. We have to sell."* So, six months down the track, we sold in a recession and lost well over a million dollars, having to sell our properties tied to the business as well.

I knew there was only one way I could go—vertical! I had to rise up and pull us out of this imploding situation. I just needed to hustle beyond all definition. I needed to pull off a freakin' miracle.

I asked myself, *"How could I make a difference, and what did I love doing?"* The answer was clear: I wanted to use my passion for training, and understanding people's behavior to help individuals become conscious, caring and successful leaders in the workplace.

I'll never forget meeting with my first potential client. It was a well-known company with 300 staff, and they had advertised for "Team Sales Training". It was a 50km (31 miles) drive so John generously offered to drive me.

The manager in charge of recruiting was a nice guy and we chatted easily; about halfway through our conversation though, he secretly confessed that he wanted to leave his job and work for me. Afterwards, I slumped back into the car dejectedly.

John sensed my obvious disillusionment and suggested we have a coffee in a nearby shopping center.

As I was consoling myself with a good dose of caffeine. I looked over and noticed a travel agency business, Harvey World Travel. A little spark kindled in my mind. I had heard that travel agencies did a lot of staff training. As I was already dressed and ready to go, I took the plunge, telling John I'd be back in a minute.

The manager was interested in my background in leadership and management and wanted to know all about our company's training style and some of the more subtle "soft skills" training we offered such as body language and language sales patterns. I felt a moment of uncertainty when she admitted that she had already spoken to a couple of training companies and wasn't sure which way she wanted to go. Then she smiled, "But I think I want to go with you!"

Next, she surprised me by doing something few people do in a first meeting: she gave me some other contacts also required staff training. I phoned every single contact that same day and over time, one lead led to another.

My first training package was $3000 per person, and I started with 30 people. By the end of that year, my company had hit one million dollars in contracts for our training.

I must admit, it does seem ironic when you think about it: to have lost one million dollars and made one million dollars all in the same year! I cried with relief, although it wasn't over, we weren't out of financial ruin—

Our accountant calculated we had to pay nearly $400,000 in tax!

Despite my disillusionment, I did know one thing—something I was doing was working. I had learned how to make money fast and how to deliver transformative education and training. I had learned how to build teams and provide them with life-affirming strategies. I had learned how to manage teams and build leaders. I earned the title the turn around Queen.

These lessons and experiences accumulated over many years and allowed me to build a successful business I even wrote a book in 2017 about the importance of first impressions in business called *The Million-Dollar Handshake* published by Hachette Australia and became a tool to help fundraise with one-third of all profits going to charities supporting orphans. (Did I mention I started my life as an orphan?) It then become business book of the year for 7Dials Orion books UK.

Igniting The Conscious Leader Within

Unfortunately, as I finished writing my second book The Conscious Leader, COVID-19 has spread throughout the world. A check recently arrived in the mail made out to me for $9,500 for a keynote talk. I had to return it to them as travel restrictions had tightened and my livelihood was on hold, all conferences cancelled. John jokes about people paying me to speak, *"I'd pay you not to!"*

But as life would have it, and all jokes aside, I find myself in another great challenge. I couldn't change this new crisis, but I could adapt and reinvent myself and my business direction. I've been through an external crisis before with the GFC, and I learned that the key to overcoming it was in my internal response.

As the great Holocaust survivor Viktor Frankl taught us and I'll say it again, *"When we are no longer able to change a situation, we are challenged to change ourselves."*[3]

Your crisis may be a global one, like the GFC or COVID19, or it may be a domestic one from within your own household, maybe an illness or death. The scale of the crisis isn't the most important factor. The most important factor is to wake up and become conscious of your options. Become aware of what you can control and how you can ignite transformation within yourself and the lives of others. *"When you believe in yourself others believe in you too"*!

.

Welcome to the decade of *The Conscious Leader where your presence matters.*

The book, *The Conscious Leader* 2021 is supporting "The Bombay Mothers And Children's Welfare Society"[2], helping disadvantaged children and families receive treatment for cancer.

[3] Frankl, Viktor. *Man's Search For Meaning*. (1st April 2008) Rider.

[2] thebmcws.com[27]

---

27. https://www.thebmcws.com

The Ultimate Rebirth

By Imani Capri

"First, pray to know your purpose, why you are here on the planet. Seek to understand that; until you know that, all other knowledge is useless."

-Danny Nagashima

Giving birth hurts. In the end the pain, the pressure and prolonged process are all worth it. The greatest irony is, many of us are born, but fewer of us actually live. The contractions, water- breaking, dilation, opening up, and pushing through the most painful experiences, ultimately lead us to birthing the life we were always meant to live.

Of the 7.8 billion people on the planet, how many are really living the life of their true purpose, happiness, and power? Are you? Have you ever felt that way? Do you feel like you are here, on the planet, but not really living the level of life that you envision and brings you joy? If so, I want to encourage you, it is never too late to be great! It is never too late to give birth to a new you and a new life that truly suits you.

I have not physically birthed any children, but I have birthed a new life, my own. As a result of having experienced almost a decade of childhood sexual abuse, I once lived feeling defeated, powerless, and unworthy, like I was a victim to my life circumstances. Today, I live a life in which I walk in purpose, power and worth.

Today, I am an empowerment speaker, on-air radio personality, published author, entrepreneur, and serious breaker – of – family – generational curses.

Today, my life is in perfect alignment with my purpose to help ignite healing, transformation, and elevation in others. However, the journey to understanding my purpose was intense. I had to be reborn in the process. Much like a woman giving birth to a child, I had to go through various stages of labor, in order to birth the life I am living now.

In child-birthing there are three main stages of labor: Contraction and Dilation, Water -Breaking and Pushing, and Afterbirth and Recovery.

The stages involved in the rebirthing of one's self are similar. In the rebirthing of one's self, the *"contractions"* that forces us to open up or shift in some way, often manifest in the form of divinely designed obstacles. Once we are presented with those divinely designed obstacles, then our lives begin to *"dilate"* as part of a process to clear out anything that could obstruct a smooth delivery. The "water-*breaking and push-through"* stage in rebirthing one's self could be likened to those pivotal, life-changing moments we experience that completely change everything. Whether those moments are subtle or abrupt, nothing is the same and we have no other way to break through, other than choosing to push through. In the *"afterbirth and recovery"* stage of rebirthing one's self, there is the recognition and releasing of all of the old things that were needed to feed the process leading up to the rebirth. In this stage, holding onto the old stuff would become toxic. Once we have released the *"afterbirth"* then we recover. *"Recovery"* begins with making the commitment to parent yourself and to nurture the needs of your new life with patience, grace and loving kindness.

Working through these three stages of rebirth have taught me two incredibly simple, yet powerful lessons:

1. *Each of us is so much more powerful than we know.*
2. *Nothing new is ever birthed from remaining the same or without enduring some level of discomfort.*

My rebirth began abruptly. The strength of the first contraction was jarring. My new life was on its way and there was no stopping it.

LABOR BEGINS WITH A CATALYST

Leaving an abusive household was the catalyst that ignited my rebirth. My heart raced as my stepfather chased me with a butcher knife. I ran to my room to get away from him. I slammed the door, raised the window and climbed into the night. In a tee shirt, shorts and barefoot, I ran to a neighbor's home to call the police. I was 20 years old. That was the first time I called the police on my mother's husband even though he had been raping me since I was 11 years old. I didn't have the courage to press charges against him that night, but I did have the courage to walk away. It wasn't easy.

The Texas summer heat simmered from the pavement beneath the soles of my bare feet, nudging me to move forward. Like an infant learning to walk, I hesitantly placed one foot in front of the other, taking my first steps out of the pain-filled prison that had become my life, toward something new. Those precious steps were crucial. They were my first steps as a woman, toward saving the wounded little girl inside of me who longed for justice and happiness. They were my first steps from darkness into the light.

That summer night, June 8, 1999, my journey toward conquering fear began. That night, the process of my transformation began. I had no real understanding of how climbing out of my bedroom window and running would lead to me discovering my purpose and my voice, but it did.

PUSH THROUGH TO BREAK THROUGH: WHEN YOU CHANGE EVERYTHING CHANGES

"The voice of a Buddha is a pure and far-reaching voice, and it is one of the Buddha's thirty-two outstanding features. The voice is the vibration of the living whole." Daisaku Ikeda

I was 19 years old the first time I heard Nam-Myoho-Renge-Kyo while watching Tina Turner's life story in the movie, *"What's Love Got To Do With It?'*

That funny sounding phrase would later come to play a hugely significant role in helping me to transform my victimhood into being victorious.

Several years later a friend introduced me to Nichiren Buddhism and the literal chanting of Nam-Myoho-Renge-Kyo. She explained that chanting would enable me to start seeing the true nature of my life and allow me to begin tapping into the vast power and potential that laid dormant in my life.

I committed to studying Nichiren Buddhism for six months before deciding to make it my primary spiritual practice. My decision to embrace Nichiren Buddhism was the "water-breaking" moment in my rebirthing process. It was the game-changing catalyst that awakened me to the fact that I had the power to change my life. It taught me that, no matter what I had gone through, my life was inherently valuable and powerful. I only needed to tap in to see that power, do the work of inner transformation and learn how to effectively direct that power.

Many times, in order for us to be reborn, we must revisit our past and take inventory of what we have been avoiding. It is the process of facing and re-purposing those old traumas and hurtful experiences, which enables us to be free to step into birthing a new self and new life. This is a gift which we are then powerful enough to give ourselves; it is not something our environment can do for us, but we do it for ourselves from the inside out.

In Nichiren Buddhism there is a concept referred to as *The Oneness of Self and the Environment*. This concept teaches that the outer environment is a reflection of the inner-self, in essence a mirror. When we create deep inner change, it is a universal law that our outer environment must also change. I took this teaching and engraved it in my heart. I used it as a compass to guide my thinking and actions. It became the key that unlocked and freed me from everything that had been holding me hostage, most of all how I had misperceived myself.

Daisaku Ikeda, President of the Soka Gakkai International expresses it best:

> *"When we change, the world changes. The key to all change is in our inner transformation – a change of our hearts and minds. This is human revolution. We all have the power to change. When we realize this truth, we can bring forth that power anywhere, anytime, and in any situation."*

With time and consistency, the changes that were occurring within me began to manifest as change in my physical environment. The changes were deep and far reaching to every area of my life; similar to a line of dominos falling once the very first one had been moved.

Those massive changes began with me having a nervous breakdown, which ultimately became a huge breakthrough. It forced me to face and heal all the years of trauma and pain that I had suppressed.

In healing from all of those emotions I began and completed several rounds of therapy and pressed legal charges against the man who abused me as a child. After two trials, he was successfully prosecuted and sentenced to more than 20 years in prison. In the midst of that, I completed a Bachelor's in Broadcast Journalism and a Master's in Digital Storytelling and Marketing.

As I worked on my healing and practiced my craft, I found my voice. I began speaking and sharing my story. I discovered my purpose, to help inspire and ignite healing and transformation in others through sharing how I was able to change my pain into power.

A new life began to blossom and flourish before my eyes.

NURTURING A NEW LIFE

As I released old wounds and disbelief in myself, tremendous changes emerged. I reconciled and transformed relationships with both of my biological parents and all five of my siblings after being estranged for more than ten years.

People reached out to book me for speaking engagements and media interviews. I was invited to contribute part of my story to a book for teen survivors of sexual abuse entitled: *Things We Haven't Said: Sexual Violence Survivors Speak Out.*

I was then approached about co-creating a radio show on a new FM station in Cleveland, Ohio called *Truth Be Told* which was dedicated to shifting the culture and conversation around all issues related to abuse and sexual violence. Upon creating that radio show I was invited to create another show called *Conversations in Courage with Imani Capri*, where I interviewed interesting people who were doing positive things with a courageous spirit all around the world.

Those shows have been on-air for more than 2 years now.

Phenomenal things continue to occur in my life today. One of the greatest experiences I have had in 2020 was being a featured speaker in the first online Power Voice Summit created by the legendary motivational speaker Les Brown and top mindset and wealth coach Jon Talarico.

The rebirthing of my new life has been and continues to be incredibly beautiful and fun!

My encouragement to you is simple:

You hold the power to change anything in your life at any time. Continue working on yourself, that is the key to manifesting everything you truly desire.

Loving yourself, healing yourself and believing in yourself, in alignment with the God of your understanding, is the greatest rebirth there is!

Contact Imani Capri for Bookings:

Email:imanicapri@gmail.com

(440) 941-0328

Follow Imani Capri:

FB: The Imani Capri Page[28]

IG:iam_imanicapri[29]

---

28. https://www.facebook.com/TheImaniCapri/

29. https://www.instagram.com/iam_imanicapri

YouTube: Imani Capri[30]

---

30. *https://www.youtube.com/user/imanicapri*

Conclusion...

Thank you for getting here.

Did you know that less than 10% of all the readers who have this book will ever read these words? Just think, that already puts you in the top 10% of the world out there!

It's clear to me that you're hungry to accomplish something amazing in your life and you're ready to leap into the next level of you.

You chose us, the authors of this book, to help you get there and for that I speak on behalf of us all when I say we're honored to have shared with you.

Our hope is that the stories contained in this book, Hunger for the Hustle Volume 1, can be fuel for whatever journey you're on.

You can pick up this book, read or re-read the tale of someone's journey from struggle to success and be ignited to take on your own challenges. As Roosevelt said,

"A smooth sea never made a skilled sailor".

Today you may be going through a storm, or maybe it'll be tomorrow, and we hope that the pearls of wisdom and steps to achievement shared in these pages can serve as a guide for you during those storms.

You should also be acknowledged for your giving heart and your generosity.

With each purchase of this book a donation is being made to the **"Beanie's Arc"**. There is a very rare cancer, rhabdomyosarcoma, that only is found in very small children and this horrible disease has struck us close to our hearts.

Rhabdomyosarcoma steals little beautiful souls away from us far too early and because of that, little is known of the cancer and even less is known about how to fight it. My co-creator of this book, Jake Fowler, has firsthand experience with this horrible disease and is dedicated to helping raise funds to find better and kinder treatment. Therefore, proceeds from your purchase of this book will be given to this foundation in hopes of preventing any more of the worlds tiniest people from being taken from us too soon.

For more information on this foundation and if you'd love to help further or know more…visit: alicesarc.org/arc/beanie-evans[31]

Again, thank you for your time and your support.

The world needs more people who believe in abundance and charity like you do.

The greatest job I have is being a Dad. And, once I became a Dad I realized one of our greatest responsibilities; to ensure we make this world a better place than we found it, so our children can thrive beyond us and pay that homage forward.

This book and all the Hunger for the Hustles to follow is a part of that legacy.

On behalf of Jake Fowler and myself, I hope you join us in forging that legacy.

-Michael Bridgman, Co-Editor and Co-Creator, Hunger for the Hustle.

"You have something special, you have GREATNESS in You" – Les Brown

---

31. https://www.alicesarc.org/arc/beanie-evans

It's Your Turn...

There is power in a great story, isn't there?

Great stories have the potential to spark us into action, action that can change our world and the world around us, the world of those we care most about.

We can find in a great story a seed of wisdom we can nurture into thriving success.

We can find in a great story the path to a better version of ourselves.

Great stories can be the lighthouse of hope we've been waiting and wanting to run towards, and they can reveal the hidden recipes to accomplish something we've been longing to do.

It is often great stories that inspire us to step up our game and start acting like the person we'd love to be.

Our hope is that these stories, the ones inside the pages of this book can ignite something with you. Something that makes you want to share your story with the world.

As one of my all-time favorite orators, Les Brown, says "You have something special you have greatness in you!" (we used this quote just before perhaps we could go with 'turn your mess into your message and your test becomes your testimony'

And... We'd like to help you achieve that greatness!

If you've ever wanted to become a published author and if you believe that your story is one that can inspire others, then we'd love to hear from you.

In fact you're exactly who we're looking for to help us create the next Hunger for the Hustle compilation book. And by purchasing this book you have gained an exclusive access to feature in future volumes!

Many of the authors in this book were friends and colleagues of Jake and I's to begin with. But there are several others who we met along our journey and are now authors in this book with us. That could be you!

To share your story with us visit: hungerforthehustle.com[32]

Click on the **"Become an Author"** button for more details.

You have a journey and a story to share, and others need to read it and hear it.

Let us help you inspire others and achieve something amazing.

---

32. http://www.hungerforthehustle.com

" TOO MANY OF US ARE NOT LIVING OUR DREAMS, BECAUSE WE'RE TOO BUSY LIVING OUR FEARS "

— Les Brown

Achieving your dreams is never an easy road. It's not supposed to be. It's supposed to challenge you in ways you could never imagine. So, how do you keep going in those challenges? **In this book you'll find 28 unique answers to that question.** You'll find **28 authors** who share their stories of 'Struggle to Success' in an effort to show you that anything is truly possible when you refuse to stop pursuing and never take no for a final answer.

From entrepreneurial advice that will help you go further in business, to **finding your passion** through adventure and exploration; from overcoming debilitating addiction to vanquishing the death knell of cancer...within these pages our hope is that you'll uncover a story that **resonates so strongly with you,** it'll re-ignite the spark of your dreams and fire up your passion for achieving greatness. What are you waiting for? Crack the spine on this book and let's get started!

STAY HAPPY | STAY HEALTHY | STAY HUNGRY & KEEP ON HUSTLING!

FEATURING CHAPTERS FROM

Beanie Marri, Aaron Cryder, Barry Overton, Beata Seweryn-Reid
Chucky Smiley, David Spencer, Denise Nicholson, Eric Collier, Fernanda Castañeda, Imani Cuori
Jade Westlake, Janet Mackay, Jay Reace, Joanna Kleier, Kasundra Brown, Keith Lloyd
Lori Bruton, Luis Sandoval, Michelle Hardy, Nelson Belitjar, Susan Russell, Tarnya Coley
Wayne Johnson, Catherine Motloy, Larry Normile, Katie Corbett, Jacob Fowler, Michael Bridgman

FOREWORD BY

Les Brown, Jon Talarico